Contents

5

1

The Reach of Human Knowing

In recent years there has been an explosion of interest in what is called ESP, or extrasensory perception. A whole set of experiences is being discovered, experiences that bring human beings knowledge in unusual ways.

Ordinarily we learn from our sight and hearing, from touch and taste and smell. Our senses are like five different kinds of radio sets hooked up to a computer. For centuries it was thought that our senses provided the primary information about the world.

Now it appears that human beings have another, entirely different, receiving set. Human beings have the ability to gather information without using the normal input channels of the senses and nervous system, and they can do this across space and time. These abilities enable people to make contact with "spiritual" or "psychic" beings, who don't seem to be material or to have physical bodies and can't be observed by our senses. Such beings are known by a variety of names—discarnate spirits, ghosts, gods and goddesses, angels and demons. Besides this, the human mind or psyche also has the power to influence other human beings and also to influence physical matter by means other than the physical. While these two abilities (psychic healing and psychokinesis) are not perceptions, they are grouped together with the other experiences known as ESP or "psi" phenomena.

Until about one hundred years ago no serious scientist considered the possibility of such a thing as ESP. For a long time it was left to people involved in the occult— people like mediums who held séances, or those who worked with magic or astrology or witchcraft. And these people had a shady reputation at best.

But this had not always been the case. Until early in the sixteenth century almost everyone, student and priest and common person alike, had been deeply interested in these strange abilities.

Then a change in outlook began to occur. What we call the scientific point of view was beginning to develop. The scientific goal was to get a clearer understanding of the world and to show that there is order in the way physical things work. And the only way to be sure of facts about the physical world is to check them over and over again through our senses.

There was much to be charted and measured and calculated, from the course of the stars, the height of mountains, the depth of oceans, to the structure of the human body itself. It is no wonder that scientists became so engrossed in spelling out facts about the world from their sense experience that they forgot there was any other way of knowing. Before too long they had managed to convince most people that there is no way to learn anything except through our senses and our reason.

These scientists thought that only superstitious people would believe that there was another, more mysterious, way of knowing. But when something of value is ignored by the leaders of a culture, it is usually taken over by out-

8

siders who are mistrusted by the "in" group. This is what happened to ESP.

But we live at the end of an era. We live at a time when science is not as sure of itself as it was 75 years ago. A great deal has been learned about the physical world that surrounds us, but the more we learn about its order and regularity, the more things we find that don't fit with the ordinary ways we perceive and experience this world of matter and space and time. Today's scientists admit that the universe seems to operate in more than one way, and that the old idea that everything is determined by one set of laws gives us only part of the picture of what really happens. In the last ten years physicists in particular have become deeply interested in the meaning of extrasensory perception for their own study.

The first serious investigation of ESP in modern times began in the late nineteenth century. It was started by a group of men, several of them at Oxford, who had a talent for scientific study. They realized that there was a large gap in our knowledge about people and the world; so they organized the Society for Psychical Research in England. The results of their work were published in *The Journal of Psychical Research*. Their painstaking investigation of experiences gathered from all kinds of people has set the standard for careful study of the subject ever since. Early in the 1900s a similar society, with similar standards and a journal, was founded in the United States. By 1930, psychical research, or parapsychology as it was sometimes called, had moved into the laboratory. With J. B. Rhine at Duke University, the study of ESP, psi experiences or parapsychology (the terms are used almost interchangeably) became an established science.

These were all men of the highest reputation. Some of them were accredited scientists. Some were even Nobel prize winners. All of them had entered the work because

9

of sincere interest and conviction. While they were at first groping in the dark, they steadily refined their methods so that ESP research has continued to improve along with the exciting developments and new techniques in other scientific fields.

This did not mean that the initial ESP research was accepted by the scientific community, however. Far from it. It created an uproar in the scientific community. Individuals were accused of being gullible, or even downright dishonest. There was practically no follow-up of the data they presented. It is true that a few outside researchers did try the methods that Rhine at Duke was finding so successful in testing people's ESP abilities. But so little was known about all the variable factors in these experiments that these efforts misfired. This only convinced more people that ESP was humbug, and hardly anyone was interested in the point of view being developed. Stanley Krippner tells the story of these early years in his absorbing personal account, *Song of the Siren.*

Scientists, it seems, can be as narrow-minded and prejudiced as the rest of us. As Kuhn points out in *The Structure of Scientific Revolutions,* they don't like change any more than other people do. But like it or not, science was already in the midst of a full-scale change, and the status of parapsychological research would soon be affected by this change.

Suddenly in 1969 the Parapsychological Association, after years of rejection, was accepted into the distinguished American Association for the Advancement of Science. Students in various fields began to show an interest in psi research. By 1972 some of the leading research institutions were starting to study these experiences that had been laughed off the stage scarcely ten years before. In 1974 Charles Panati, formerly chief physicist for RCA and now a science editor for *Newsweek* magazine, brought

10

out an excellent survey of the experimental work being done in parapsychology. He concluded his introduction with these words:

> The computer age began in the 1950s, the space age in the 1960s, and the psychic age has begun in the 1970s. Paranormal phenomena are no longer being viewed as impossible things. They have finally moved off the magician's stage and come full swing into the scientific laboratory. What is happening there, and its implications for dramatically reshaping our image of ourselves and our place in the universe, are the subjects of this book.[1]

ESP or psi has at last achieved scientific respectability, and these experiences need to be dealt with open-mindedly, especially by people who are interested in the church and theology.

A Changing World and ESP

For a long time we humans were comfortable in a world that seemed solid and understandable. We thought we knew how many elements this world was made of, and we believed that the different atoms stayed put and didn't fly off into energy or change into other kinds of matter. They followed laws based on the work of Sir Isaac Newton. Man seemed to have the upper hand because he could study things out and predict what ought to be done. Darwin had even charted the laws that give us our place in this world. He showed how natural selection works so that only the fittest and the most adaptable survive.

All of these laws, of course, appeared to work blindly. In addition, these laws seemed to show beyond any doubt that everything which touches man, inside or out, is purely physical. If there is nothing but matter stretching out in every direction, then there is nothing else to affect matter

11

but other matter. According to this point of view, we are shut up inside a physical universe where no experience can reach us except through our senses. And if sense experience is the only contact we have with the world, it is absurd to imagine that we have any experience like ESP.

Christian theology also gave in to this point of view. There was no real argument. God was immanent in these processes in the physical world. He could be known in history. But it was considered foolish to dream of direct experiences of God or any kind of extrasensory perception. A few like Swedenborg and the Cambridge Platonists believed something different, but they were out of step, and the parade passed them by. This attitude prevailed until the end of the nineteenth century.

Then overnight, here and there, a new breed of student began to discover strange bits of information about this seemingly solid, unchanging earth. Becquerel discovered rays (or radiation) that exposed tightly sealed photographic plates and encouraged Marie Curie to investigate the substance. She found that somehow uranium was constantly bombarding itself and finally broke down into lead and another highly active substance—radium.

Scarcely fifty years later we were beginning to realize that *no* matter is solid, that even the most primary atom is composed of particles that seem to revolve about a center. For a while the discovery of new particles grew at an almost alarming rate, until now more than two hundred tiny charges or subatomic particles have been discovered.

As if this were not enough to wipe out the solid ground under our feet, Einstein showed that the familiar laws of Newton's physics are only partially true. These laws do not give us certainty, particularly about things that go on below the surface in this world.

Another round of discoveries has been made by modern biologists and anthropologists who find that living things don't evolve as simply as we had thought. Development often comes in great leaps, through mutation; and for various reasons, survival of the fittest just doesn't account for all the forms of life, particularly human ones. This point of view has been expressed by Loren Eiseley and Teilhard de Chardin.

Still another blow to the old order came from the work of depth psychologists and students of psychosomatic medicine. They have found that physical health is deeply influenced by a person's state of mind, by emotions, and even by one's attitude of faith and hope. Doctors have begun to realize that germs and drugs are not the only things that affect our health. Something as intangible, as immaterial, as finding meaning in one's life can make the difference between health and disease, while lack of meaning and purpose can tip the scales from life towards death.

Last of all, the increasing volume of evidence about extrasensory phenomena has begun to carry weight on its own as these experiences have been duplicated in one laboratory after another.

Thus, step by step, scientists have knocked the props out from under our orderly world. These technicians, whose job it is to look at facts, have come to see evidence of something more than matter acting and developing mechanically. Although many theologians, along with the behavioral psychologists and a few social scientists, are still caught in the materialist point of view, other serious scientists have broken with this thinking. Recent polls show how much the ideas of the scientific community, and also of the general public, have changed in the last ten years.

Space scientists have also become interested in ESP. On July 28, 1975, the *Los Angeles Times* ran a front page feature article on the subject. The story gave a clear understanding of psi research, and reported that astronaut Edgar

Mitchell, who has walked on the moon, has retired from the space program to found an organization for the study of these experiences and related mental phenomena. The group is called the Institute of Noetic Sciences, which simply refers to mental perceptions, particularly apart from the senses.

The way scientists and other students of ESP see it, every human being has two different ways of taking in information or two different ways of knowing:

First, there is the familiar way of letting our senses tell us about the world. This way gives us information which is not too hard to verify as long as we stay with measurable quantities and don't get into qualities of experience.

But the idea that this is the only way of knowing has had a spotty history. It was first stated definitely by Aristotle, and later among Christians in the Arian heresy. It was mostly dormant until Aristotle's thinking was discovered by Islam and passed on to Western Europe to be adopted into Christianity by Thomas Aquinas, and ultimately refined and handed on by Descartes. But in both ancient and medieval times most thinkers recognized that their task was to learn about this way of acquiring knowledge, not to establish it as the only way of knowing.

Not until almost the nineteenth century did it occur to serious thinkers to suggest that the idea of learning anything through extrasensory experiences was ridiculous. Gradually, however, the emphasis on sense experience increased until in the 1700s a thinker like Immanuel Kant could make fun of dreamers who claimed to "see" ghosts. Kant wrote a book titled *Dreams of a Ghost-Seer* to ridicule Swedenborg because that philosopher-theologian had described his clairvoyant experience of seeing Stockholm in flames although he was many miles away from the city at the time the great conflagration occurred. Because clair-

14

voyance looked like an impossibility to Kant, he tried to persuade people that Swedenborg was an old fool.

The second way of knowing, one that bypasses the senses, appears to be equally real. It can give knowledge of either the physical world or of things that do not seem to be physical (whatever that word may mean in the light of modern physics).

These experiences have two possibilities that seem strange to us. Something nonphysical can touch human personality and thus bring about action in the ordinary material world. Or, a human personality itself can reach out and touch both human beings and nonhuman materials by some power unlike any kind of known physical energy. In this way the human psyche can have a noticeable effect on material objects and, particularly through healing, on other human beings.

This kind of ability, on either the giving or the receiving end, is not shared equally by all human beings. It is found in a noticeable degree in only a few individuals. But modern research has shown that most of us have some of this kind of power, or at least more of it than we ordinarily realize.

Thus, we human beings have two ways of receiving input from the world, and two realms within this world to receive it from. And by some similar means we also have two ways of reaching out to change the world, and two different realms in the world in which to intervene.

As strange as it seems to us who have been taught to use only one kind of experience, this understanding of another way of knowing has had a long and honorable history. Almost all pre-modern religions have held this view. The best documented studies of earlier religions show how widespread this understanding has been.

Mircea Eliade documents this basic view in his monumental work, *Shamanism*. His book, which includes fifty

15

pages of bibliographical references, shows that shamanism with this understanding of human knowing has been found in every part of the globe in a way hardly explainable by cultural influence. The same point of view is well known in America today through books on Indian culture like Neihardt's *Black Elk Speaks,* Franc Newcomb's *Hosteen Klah: Navaho Medicine Man,* and *Lame Deer, Seeker of Visions.* It is even better known through the works of Carlos Castaneda, best sellers on most college campuses. *The Teachings of Don Juan, A Separate Reality, Journey to Ixtlan,* and *Tales of Power* are required reading if one wants to keep up with the interests, attitudes, and direction of the younger generation. These works of popular anthropology speak of experiences which are described in various scientific studies.

Much of the present-day interest in drugs among young people springs from their attempt to find some way of reaching beyond ordinary perception, as Andrew Weil has pointed out in *The Natural Mind.* Youth and even older individuals have turned to drugs to find access to another realm of reality. The church once provided such access, but it no longer does, and probably the best way to eliminate drug abuse is not so much to prohibit it as to provide legitimate ways of experiencing this other reality.

Plato still offers some of the most readable and best thought-out presentations of the two ways of knowing. His works were helpful to the early Christian fathers in expressing their understanding of the two realms of reality that can be known in two different ways. Justin Martyr, Irenaeus, Tertullian, Basil, Chrysostom, Ambrose, Augustine—all shaped Christian thinking so that it survived through the centuries. They all held this basic point of view of the two ways of knowing, which has continued in the Eastern Orthodox Church to the present time.

The understanding of another realm of reality is found

16

in nearly all Oriental religions, and in the Chinese scripture known as the *I Ching* or *Book of Changes* there is full expression of the idea that human beings can reach out in two ways to two different realities. The *I Ching* is used by many college students almost as a handbook of experience. More often, however, Oriental religion stops with the idea that there is only one reality, and that is the reality of another world and another way of knowing. Hinduism and Buddhism accept the idea of the human capacity to reach out beyond the physical world, but then they seem to conclude that there is little need to relate this to the material world because they appear to consider this physical world an illusion and unreal.

In our time the basic point of view which acknowledges two realities and two ways of knowing them has been revived by the new medical specialty of psychiatry, largely through the work of Sigmund Freud, Carl Jung, and their followers. The most complete understanding of this view is provided by Jung, who believed that individuals can learn to use both ways of knowing, and that until we do begin to use them both, we cannot know what either reality is like in itself. Jung believed that we have to keep both feet firmly on the ground, one in either world, to see clearly what is real in either of the two worlds.

Christianity and the Ways of Knowing

Modern Christians have different attitudes about our ways of knowing reality. Some people simply hope the problem of ESP will go away. Some biblical critics also are guilty of this. They ignore all parts of the Bible that tell about experiences which could be called extrasensory or paranormal or psi phenomena. Things like prophecy, healing, miracles, dreams, visions, and straight extrasensory experiences of clairvoyance or precognition are not considered important enough to bother with. So these critics pretend they aren't there or that the biblical writers were talking about something else.

Secondly, there are Christians who frankly say that the only way any significant knowledge comes to us is through our five senses. This includes nearly all Christian theologians since the Enlightenment, certainly the leading ones like Schleiermacher, Kierkegaard, Harnack, Troeltsch. The same attitude persists among almost all modern theologians, as John Macquarrie demonstrates in *Twentieth-Century Religious Thought*. The most daring, as well as the most honest and consistent, is Rudolf Bultmann. He says outright that it is "mythology" pure and simple to believe that men can be influenced by anything outside their physical, material environment. By calling such a belief in healing or miracles or the like "mythological" Bultmann was saying in a nice way that this belief is unscientific, wish-fulfilling, and probably superstitious nonsense.

Urban Holmes, dean of the theological school at the University of the South, follows the same line. He cannot understand how there could be any knowledge which does not come from something physical. He writes:

> Yet I am not certain how the subject knows this [spiritual] reality or what it is apart from images of objects, which are in some sense physical. I am puzzled as to how one is called to attend to this reality, unless his central nervous system is stimulated by some bit of sense data, even if it is only the electrical current measurable by an EEG. It is completely baffling to me how there can be knowledge without the intentional act of knowing, which is at some level of awareness (perhaps "tacit knowing"), be it differentiated or undifferentiated.[2]

The same point of view was expressed twenty years earlier by F. R. Tennant in his *Philosophical Theology*. Tennant suggested that "Such immediate *rapport* between God and the human soul as theism asserts, cannot be discerned with (psi) immediacy . . . nor can any transcendent faculty, mediating such contact, be empirically traced."[3]

In order to understand and use the New Testament, according to Bultmann and his followers, we have to strip it of a good share of its contents, all the mythological elements, all the stories of psi or ESP experiences. "Demythologized" is the way Bultmann put it. Probably he was right about the need to interpret older religious works in language and ideas modern people can accept, but Bultmann was one hundred years behind the times. He tried to promote a world view many people had already outgrown, and he did not sense how far the modern world had progressed. The experiences he wanted to delete from the New Testament are the very ones many scientists are reaching out to understand. Even more important, they are also the ones through which young people are beginning to find religious meaning.

Besides these two, there is a third attitude, which tries to get the best of both worlds. This was the point of view Luther and Calvin held, and it was revived in recent times by Karl Barth. Barth believes that all kinds of miraculous things happened in New Testament times. God broke his own laws to come into the physical world and let men see what could happen. Once the world knew about the revelation of Jesus Christ, there was no more need for parapsychological events. God used them only to get people to take the church seriously, and now one can only have faith that God has the power to make them happen, because they don't happen any more.

In this way Barth could have the best of two worlds. He could be respected as an orthodox Christian who held to the truth of the Bible. And at the same time he could be respected in scientific circles for his sophisticated and enlightened understanding that in this world humans are confined within a purely physical and even mechanical system. Barth was cheating.

More recently a fourth point of view about these experiences has risen among many conservative Christians, both fundamental and pentecostal. They recognize that there are such things as fortunetelling and astrology and ESP, and that occasionally they bring true knowledge. But either these things are seen as gifts coming directly from God, or else they are considered to come from Satanic powers and to be evil. Thus, if one happens to have precognitive powers or ability as a medium and is not connected with a church of orthodox belief, then the power must come from the Devil.

This is the view of many leaders of the recent charismatic movement such as Dennis Bennet, Derek Prince, and Don Basham. They acknowledge that psi events occur today, and that they are sometimes actual gifts of the Spirit. When they are found outside the circle of orthodox belief, however, they can only be the work of the Evil One, which will damage anyone who comes into contact with it.

According to this view, a person who innocently came into contact with these experiences before being converted to orthodox Christianity can be haunted even after conversion. The only solution then is for the person to admit his guilt and to submit to the ministry of deliverance or exorcism. Nearly all mental and physical ills are attributed to the activity of demons, and traffic with the "occult" or parapsychological experience is understood as one of the common ways of being infected. According to this point of view, one visit to a fortuneteller could make problems for a person for a lifetime and for their innocent children and families. Even scientific study of ESP is considered unwise, if not catastrophic.

Finally, there is the view that extrasensory perception is a natural part of human knowing which the modern world gradually forgot in its effort to develop as much objective understanding as possible. Most people have some sensitivity to this non-sensory kind of knowing, and it can probably be developed in all but a very few of us. On the other hand, only a few rare individuals have great gifts in this area.

From this point of view such a gift is understood as natural and morally neutral. Like the gift of a great singing voice or an ability to make money, it may be used for good or for evil, *for God* or *for the Evil One*. The importance of ESP and parapsychological abilities is in what they tell us about the capacities of human beings. These very capacities can point the way to an understanding of classical Christianity and help modern Christians grasp the power of that Christianity and to share in it.

This last is the basic view we shall consider, looking first at what is meant by psi or ESP and some of the recent data which demonstrates its reality. We shall next go into the different ways in which these experiences of psi come to people. Then we shall consider some of the experiences of these phenomena as they occur in the Bible and the early church. This will bring us to a consideration of evil and to the question of how we can decide whether such experiences are good or evil, or simply neutral. To answer this question, we shall examine a model of the world that has a place for ESP and for God and for Evil. We shall conclude with a final assessment of the importance and place of ESP for Christian thought and practice today.

21

2

What Is ESP?

Is there actually information or knowledge that comes to us from some source which bypasses our five senses? It was hardly possible for people to ask this question until they had learned something about the way knowledge comes through sensory experiences. In order to consider and try to understand *extra*sensory perception, people had to have some understanding of the way knowledge is received through sensory means. The problem was much like that of understanding the unconscious. Only after Descartes had tried to define consciousness clearly for the first time in 1619 could people begin to speak of the *un*conscious and seek to learn about it.

The trouble is that our senses seem to be almost too convincing. As we have seen, almost everyone came to believe that this is the only way we get knowledge. Until 1960 no serious scientist, except for a handful of students like Jung, Rhine, and the few in Psychical Research, showed interest in anything but sense experience. Today, however, one can maintain this position only by ignoring the data about non-sensory experience and relying on *faith* (in the sense of belief without evidence) in the proposition that we can receive knowledge only through our five senses.

I am reminded of my father who was a capable chemist of the nineteenth century school of science. When he was presented with the idea of hypnotism, he recognized that he might have to change his whole frame of reference to the world if he admitted that hypnotism was real. Such an experience did not fit with his world view, and rather than give up his faith in that view of the world, he simply avoided ever being exposed to a demonstration of hypnosis.

We do not know enough about the way sensation produces knowledge to maintain this kind of faith. Scientists, it is true, have pieced together considerable information about the mechanics of sensory experience. They can explain *what* happens in sight and hearing, describing the light and sound waves that are picked up and responded to. They have learned about the chemicals that set off taste and smell, and they can picture in detail the chain of nerves that pick up information from touching objects. Science can help us follow each of these impulses to the brain and almost "see" the storage depots and how the mechanism known as remembering functions.

It is one thing, however, to treat the function of human sensation like describing a game of billiards. Once the idea of hitting a few balls around comes into someone's mind, we can show very competently what happens next. The movements of hand and eye and cue can be explained in terms of space and time and the physical properties of matter. But *how* these responses are translated into *knowing* is quite a different matter. How this process of transmitting information—which starts with bits of matter influencing other pieces of matter, such as our eyes or ears —ends up as knowledge in someone's brain is one of the great mysteries.

Efforts to explain our knowing only on a rational basis present practically insurmountable difficulties. Imagine a computer able to recall not just straight data, but all the emotional qualities of sights and sounds, of movement and touch and sometimes even taste and smell, that can come back to us. And this is one of the lesser problems in understanding the knowing that comes through our senses.

In extrasensory perception there is the additional problem that no one has any real understanding of even the mechanics of these experiences. They do not fit the world of space and time, and we seem to have no organ for taking them in and experiencing them. Clairvoyance acts as if space did not exist. Telepathy seems to put different human minds in direct touch with each other so that they share information without using any sensory capacities. Precognitive experiences apparently ignore clock time and sometimes tell about things that have not as yet happened.

Besides these, there are experiences which seem to give us knowledge of angelic and demonic powers and about those who have died. There are even experiences which appear to show the universe as it really is and reveal to some people its essential care and meaning. And then there are experiences of psychokinesis and healing in which, through human will and psychic power, one can influence other living beings and matter without touching or coming into contact with them. None of these fall within the field of ordinary sense experience or appear like ordinary human actions.

In looking at these experiences we shall not try to consider all of the data that is available. In the last few years experiments have been repeated and refined and tried again and again until there is enough evidence to fill several books. What I shall do is give samples of this evidence, selecting those that are the most interesting and the most convincing. In this way I hope to show that there actually is data here which needs to be dealt with by thinking people and particularly by religious people. For those who wish more information and who want to know more about the current experiments, there are several excellent books.[1] Let's take a look now at the variety of evidence that is found, taking up each area of ESP experience.

Clairvoyance

One of my early memories is of hearing my mother tell about an ESP experience she had had as a teen-ager. She had been dating a young man, and in the middle of one night she was awakened out of a sound sleep and seemed to see him standing at the foot of her bed. He appeared to be calling for help. She glanced at a clock. It was 2:00 A.M. The next day she learned that 24 hours earlier the young man had found out he had tuberculosis. And at 2:00 that morning he had shot himself.

Needless to say, this story made quite an impression on me. Although my scientific father ridiculed the story, I could not forget it. I had never known my mother to distort the truth, and later when I heard other similar stories, I began to realize that these experiences could be taken seriously. Technically this experience might be called telepathic, indicating communication between two minds. But like most of these experiences, there was probably some overlap between areas of communication and the information came through both clairvoyance and telepathy.

Many biologists and physicists have come to realize that lower forms of life and even matter are influenced in ways that we humans are unable to understand. Frank Brown, a tireless researcher into the rhythms of all life, has come to believe that the old scientific attempt to keep living things protected from changes in light, temperature, humidity, pressure, etc., simply does not work. Changes in tides, sunspots, electromagnetic fields, for instance, can break through the tightest controls and interrupt otherwise "constant conditions."

In one study Brown brought oysters from the Eastern seacoast to his laboratory above Lake Michigan. For a few days they continued to open and close according to the Atlantic tidal pattern they had known. Then the experiment seemed to have failed. Their rhythm altered. But it was found that the oysters, nearly 1000 miles from the sea and protected even from the light of the moon, had adjusted to the lunar rhythm in their new location. They were opening and closing by what the tide would have been if it could have washed across the land to the streets of Evanston, Illinois.

Clairvoyant experiences in human beings seem even more mysterious and harder for most of us to accept. In Monrovia, California, I came to know a man who had written one of the earliest thoughtful works on clairvoyance and telepathy, the book *Mental Radio*. Upton Sinclair was one of the most honest and forthright individuals I have known. He told me about his wife, Mary Craig Sinclair, and how she could reproduce a drawing made out of her sight, sometimes by having it placed on her body, sometimes without any contact. He also described how she was able to "see" details on a postcard hidden in a visitor's pocket, and how they had experimented for three years as carefully as possible to test her abilities. What he told me was convincing, but I did not learn until later how central the experiences of Upton and Mary Sinclair were to the whole investigation of parapsychology.

Mental Radio, in which their experiments are described, was printed and distributed privately in 1930.[2] Soon afterward, William McDougall, who had come from Oxford via Harvard to accept the chair of psychology at Duke University, came to California to learn more about Mary

Sinclair's strange abilities. Before he left, after six sessions with her, he told her that he had made a decision. His first action at Duke would be to establish a department of parapsychology. And when he did so, of course, the man he named to head the research was J. B. Rhine.

Rhine soon began to discover that college students could guess the turn of a card, and that they could do it at a rate of more than a million to one better than chance. He also discovered that interest in the experiment could definitely influence a person's capacity to see through space and tell what symbol would come up next. As long as the idea is exciting, this clairvoyant ability stays high. But let the experimenter become bored, and it declines sharply. When other people tried Rhine's experiments and failed to reach similar results, it appears that they were overlooking this important variable factor. In addition, Rhine was using cards with sets of five ordinary geometric symbols, and later researchers found that using pictures like brightly colored animals could greatly enhance this ability.

Since that time similar experiments have been carried out in all parts of the world, many of them in Soviet Russia. There is no question that some human beings possess unusual powers of seeing the unseen, as if space and intervening matter did not exist. It also appears that most of us have this capacity to some extent. Almost everyone knows the experience of driving an unfamiliar road and suddenly coming over a hilltop to recognize the landscape as if one had been there before. This experience of finding that something entirely new is suddenly as familiar as an old shoe is called a *déjà vu,* the French words for "already seen."

Out-of-the-body-experiences are another way things are revealed clairvoyantly. Several researchers have worked with people who feel that they sometimes step out of their bodies, leaving their sensory apparatus behind, and still

28

"see" things that are going on in other places. In technical psi jargon these experiences are known as OOBEs. The individuals have been asked to read and remember a many-digit number lying on a platform hung from the ceiling high above them, or sometimes to describe things in other parts of the laboratory. And some of them have been able to do so with uncanny accuracy.

One member of my own family has had this experience. He was already asleep late one night when I was called to the bedside of a critically ill parishioner whom I shall speak of as Scott. He knew Scott and knew that he was sick, but at that moment only the hospital knew that the monitoring equipment showed the vital signs slipping away.

The next morning, before I had even thought of calling the hospital, this family member came into the room and asked, "How is Scott by now?" When I questioned him, he told me, "I woke up last night, and I could see myself in bed. But then I went over near the hospital, and Scott was coming towards me. He was trying to decide whether to leave his body for good or not."

Dr. Charles Tart, a leading expert on altered states of consciousness, has written extensively about this kind of perplexing experience. Some of his most interesting work of this kind has been done with a Virginia businessman named Robert Monroe, who has described his experiences in the book, *Journeys Out of the Body.*

Some people are able to touch or simply come close to a substance, without seeing it, and tell what color it is, and it appears that blind people can often be trained in this ability, known as *derma vision.* Particular work has been done on this clairvoyant capacity in Russia, and also by Dr. Thelma Moss at the Center for Health Studies in Los Angeles. Dr. Moss worked with a woman who is totally blind, who learned to detect several different colors. She is apparently a person with a sense of humor, and her best trials have been with handling nylon panties, especially with observers taking part in the repartee.

The controversial Uri Geller is one of the most gifted living psychics. His ability to pass his hands, inches away, over a set of sealed aluminum cans and tell which one contains an object defies chance performance somewhere in the billions to one. Magicians have often claimed that his feats are a fraud and that they could duplicate the same effect. But at the Max Planck Institute in Munich and at Stanford Research Institute in Menlo Park, California, top flight scientists have worked with Geller under rigid laboratory controls and are convinced that his talents are genuine. His capacities do vary, however, with his emotional frame of mind.

Another fascinating clairvoyant ability is water-dowsing, long doubted in Western culture. But this way of finding water, by letting a forked stick turn in the dowser's hands at the right spot, is receiving careful study. In Russia it has become an established part of Soviet science. One Russian study has involved a 12-year-old boy who became quite famous in 1963 when it was found that he could discover water at great depths. He told the scientists that he could see it shimmer like green moonlight.

Another of the most interesting and least understood of these capacities is known as *psychometry*. A person with this ability can touch some object or article belonging to an unknown individual and give enough description to identify the person and even tell his whereabouts. One of the most famous psychometrists today is Olof Jonsson who has worked with the police both in this country and in his native Sweden, where he had identified at least one murderer by holding in his hands a weapon dropped by the assailant. In Chicago he was called in to help find three missing girls. He was given articles found in their abandoned car, and touching them while in a trance, he correctly stated that the girls were alive, described how they had dyed and restyled their hair, and named the town where they would be found.

There is some evidence that even ordinary people can learn to develop clairvoyant capacities like these. Russell Targ, a physicist with Stanford Research, has devised a method of training which allows a person to try to anticipate a machine's random choice from a series of pictures without being forced to make wild guesses or jump to make a decision each time. One man, whose background and personality gave no suggestion of such ability, continued to improve until he ran his scores up to a billion to one over the probability of pure chance. Targ has found that a few people have this unsuspected capacity to use clairvoyance to a remarkable degree.

Telepathy

Nearly everyone has had some experience like going to the phone to call a friend, only to have the phone ring and hear that friend's voice on the line. Or, someone we have not heard from for a long time puts a letter in the mail to us at the very time we are writing to that person. When I was first living away from home, across the country, I found that all I had to do was to get sick or upset, and invariably my mother would call from home to ask if I was well or if something was wrong.

A number of studies have been made of the capacity of human beings to relate to each other in this way. Dr. Berthold Schwarz, a New Jersey psychiatrist, was shaken by how often his child seemed to anticipate his needs. He began to record these events and to study the same capacity in other families. The results are set down in his book *Parent-Child Telepathy.* Another set of case studies is found in the work of Vincent and Margaret Gaddis, *The Curious World of Twins*. They give varied examples of the close relation between twins, who were so tuned in to one another that when one became sick, the other was stricken too, but not for a physical reason. Another case is that of identical twins, both mentally ill and in a mental hospital, who were so close that when one girl died, hospital authorities feared for the life of the other, and found that she too had just died, curled up in the same position.

Some of the most fascinating work on telepathy has been done by Montague Ullman and Stanley Krippner at New York's Maimonides Hospital. They brought people into the laboratory to sleep to discover if dreams are influenced by telepathy. In one part of the lab a "sender" concentrated on a picture, trying to transmit it to a dreamer. In other rooms the sleepers were hooked up to an electroencephalograph which shows when a dream is occurring. They were awakened at the right time and asked to tell about their dream. An elaborate system of choosing the picture made sure that no one could know the target until it was being "sent." In addition, the dream reports were recorded on tape and judged by an outside group who compared them with a whole series of pictures without knowing which one had been the target.

The "hits" were so striking that the researchers published their work in *Dream Studies and Telepathy*, published by the Parapsychology Foundation of New York. But besides this some of the "misses" turned out to be equally interesting. Every now and then a dream report told about some event that was happening in one of the researchers' lives, or something connected with one of the lab assistants. We shall look further at dreams as channels of psi influences in the next chapter.

There are equally interesting studies of a person's emotional responses to a thought in another person's mind. In one of these the "sender" was given a set of unfamiliar names. Some of them were charged with meaning for the receiver, while others were taken at random from the telephone book. As the sender turned the names up one by one and concentrated on them, the receiver simply sat in another room having the flow of blood in his index finger measured. This is done unobtrusively by a plethysmograph that shines a light through the fingertip and records the volume of blood continuously. When the agent was trying to transmit a name that had no meaning for the person on the receiving end, the blood flow fluctuated quite normally. But as soon as a name with emotional content came up, the change in blood flow was noticeable. Although the person being tested was not aware that he was reacting at all, the change in volume of blood was enough to indicate a definite emotional response. It appears that we human beings are far more sensitive to one another than we usually realize.

Animals seem to have similar sensitivity, and in Russia this fact has been put to military use. When a submarine was to be submerged and out of contact for a time, the Russians have experimented with the telepathic sensitivity of rabbits. A new-born litter of rabbits was placed aboard the sub, while the mother was kept at home base in a laboratory with electrodes implanted in her brain. Periodically one of the baby rabbits aboard the sub was killed, and at that moment the fact was recorded in the laboratory by an abrupt change in the brain waves of the mother. Telepathic communication to a living creature was able to get through from the bottom of the ocean where no physical method that we know of could reach back to land.

The work of Clive Backster on the sensitivity of plants to threat has raised a storm of controversy. Scientists may not question the methods of Backster, who is highly respected as a polygraph or lie detector expert, but they will not accept his idea that plants have emotions or experiences. Yet his tests apparently show just that.

He was playing with an interesting idea the first time, trying to determine if a plant would show on the polygraph how water moved up from soil to leaf. When there was no reaction, he tried to shock the leaf into reacting, first by dipping it into hot coffee. Then as he was deciding to get a match and burn it, the tracing jumped and kept taking upward swings.

In testing this result, Backster found that various plants responded in the same way to thoughts of damaging them. They also reacted to the sudden destruction of life, for instance, when live shrimp were dropped into boiling water in a room nearby. These responses, checked out by several investigators, happen in spite of the fact that plants have no known cells or apparatus for sensing things.

There seems to be some immediate communication between living things, some direct connection without going through the sense organs or the nervous system. Unquestionably human beings have as much potential for experience of this kind as rabbits and plants.

Precognition

There is something mind-boggling about the idea that some people are able to see into the future. It is hard enough to realize that space may not be the reality we have thought, but time seems inexorable. Yet if Einstein was on the right track in describing the relativity of time, it may not be so surprising to consider that we have capacities not limited by space and time.

Still, what bothers us is not so much the *fact* of being able to see into the future. It is more the *idea* of not being able to depend on something so familiar as time.

History gives us stories of important people who had

warnings of impending disaster. Only a few days before his death, Abraham Lincoln dreamed of getting up in deathlike stillness and going downstairs to hear muffled sounds of grief all around him. Finally he came to the East Room to find a casket guarded by soldiers and a crowd of mourners, and when he asked who had died, he was told that the President had been assassinated. Only the night before the assassination he dreamed of sailing in a ghostly vessel towards a dark and shadowy shore.

Events like these are also found in the Bible. Most of us who take these stories seriously are not surprised to realize that his precognitive abilities got Joseph out of prison in Egypt. He could tell Pharaoh's butler and baker what would happen, and when Pharaoh finally sent for him to interpret the dreams of fat and lean things, Joseph predicted the famine and suggested what to do about it. He was then put in charge of the project. Some students of the New Testament are convinced that Jesus had accurate knowledge about his death and spoke of it to his disciples.

People are naturally curious about what the future may bring. Fortune-tellers have always had a brisk trade, even though intelligent people usually scoff at their predictions. Some psychics like Jeanne Dixon have had some impressive hits. The problem is that they also miss, and it is difficult to know whether a hit or a miss is coming up and what the odds against chance really are.

There are also many who consult astrologers to predict future events in their lives on the basis of nothing more than a horoscope. Vernon Clark, a psychologist, studied twenty astrologers and is now quite convinced of their abilities. While his control group made only chance scores on identifying the information asked about, the astrologers scored at least 100 to 1 over chance, and sometimes answered every question correctly.

These were tests after the fact, however, and it is difficult to design an experiment that will test precognitive ability. But Helmut Schmidt who succeeded Dr. Rhine at Duke University has done just this. Dr. Schmidt, a well-trained physicist, in his experiment uses one of the basic discoveries of modern physics, the fact that radioactive decay is one of the most random events known. We know how many years it will take for one half of such a substance to disintegrate, but there is no way to determine which atom will give up its energy next.

Schmidt uses the decay of strontium 90 to turn on one of four colored lights in a random sequence that cannot be determined before it happens. The eleven college students in his group tried to follow their best hunches and guess which light the radioactive pile would turn on next. Out of one run of more than 10,000 precognitive "guesses" the results were better than chance by more than 1000 to 1. The three who apparently had a special knack of precognitive intuition were then run through 60,000 trials and came up with scores at odds against chance of two billion to one. Later trials with individuals especially sensitive to this kind of experience produced even higher scores.

At Maimonides Hospital in New York, Charles Honorton worked with a well-known psychic who was asked to dream on alternate nights of a picture that would be chosen at random on the following day. On five nights out of eight he was successful, but on the other eight nights, when he was shown a picture and even sound effects and asked to dream about it, he showed no talent at all for directing his dreams consciously.

Even hamsters have been shown to have precognitive ability. This work was run and recorded mechanically without human supervision, so that nothing human could interfere. One by one the hamsters were given a choice of hopping back and forth between two cages while one or the other was given an electric charge in a random pattern. The computer made sure that there was no possibility of "learning" which cage to avoid, and yet the little animals succeeded in avoiding the shock far better than could be accounted for by chance.

E. Douglas Dean, an engineer and student of psi, believes that successful businessmen are probably using precognitive talents, and that they are at least as smart in this area as hamsters. In one experiment he selected a group of successful businessmen and a control group who had shown little ability in the business world. He asked each of them to try to guess a ten-digit number which would be selected by the computer at random on the following day. The individuals who had been successful in the business world scored about ten percent better than chance. Those with average ability came out almost equal to chance, while a few of the subjects consistently guessed wrong. They seemed to lack ability in both fields, and even to show a kind of "talent" for negative precognition.

Visions of the Cosmos

The non-sensory experiences we have discussed can be checked, and we know that they often give valid information, although they give it in ways we are not able to understand. All attempts to describe these experiences in physical ways, or as some kind of subtle sensation, have failed. As Charles Panati concludes, "If anything is clear from parapsychological research, it is that known electromagnetic carriers are not the messengers of paranormal information. All attempts to understand psychic events in terms of the well-known body fields have intrinsic and intractable problems." [3]

There are certain other non-sensory experiences, however, which suggest that there is an explanation, but one on a completely different level. These are the dreams, visions, and intuitions of some people that speak of another level of reality. Among mystics and mediums and in most religious literature there is an interest in this other level of reality. These sources offer remarkably consistent descriptions of it, and they suggest that many non-sensory experiences may be given by such a reality from beyond the physical world.

As we turn to consider these experiences, it is well to remember the general tendency today to deny that there is any reality behind them. Those who deny the existence of such a reality generally forget that it is up to them to prove that it does not exist, and this is very tricky. In fact the only way to prove this is to demonstrate that one knows all there is to know about the world and has left no stone unturned where such a reality could lie hidden from view. When the best of physicists simply say they do not know that much about the world, it seems rather silly for any of the rest of us to be so dogmatic, particularly on the basis of a discarded physical theory.

At certain critical times in life, some people seem to be given a visionary glimpse into the universe as a whole, or sometimes into the depth of one aspect of it. The book of Revelation in the Bible is one record of such a view. Many of the great mythologies undoubtedly originated in this way, as well as most of the greatest religious poetry. Dante's *Divine Comedy* is not only truly superb poetry but also one of the greatest expressions of just such a vision.[4] The incomparable "Stanzas of the Soul" by St. John of the Cross and "The Hound of Heaven" by Francis Thompson are also classic expressions of this kind of visionary experience. Such experiences also come to many ordinary people who are striving to become whole and integrate their lives around a coherent meaning. The experiences are just as valid and memorable although they are not set down with such artistic talent.

In recent years I have come across three present-day descriptions of such visionary revelations, all of them matter-of-fact. The most impressive is a vision Dr. C. G. Jung had while recovering from a nearly fatal illness in which he experienced something beyond physical life. In it he found himself released from his body and soaring into the heavens. He describes how the earth looked from above, and then how he was taken onto a tremendous rock like a meteorite, carved into a temple within. As he walked up the steps, all that had been Carl Jung seemed to slough away, leaving no desires or wants or regrets, and yet he felt that he still had everything. It seemed that all his questions about his life were to be answered in the temple when a figure he knew came towards him, a man delegated to tell him that he had no right to leave earth yet but was "condemned" to return to his life. Then he awoke feeling keen disappointment. This experience, which Jung described as the most certain and solid and real of his life, is found in the chapter "Visions" in his *Memories, Dreams, Reflections.*

A similar experience was described by Arthur Ford in *The Life Beyond Death,* a posthumous work edited and introduced by Jerome Ellison. He too was near death, in a hospital in Florida, and he seemed to be separated from his body, and then to enter another realm of existence. His description has much in common with that of Jung, as if both men were describing the same reality, seen from a somewhat different aspect or angle. Ford described meeting people he had known, and coming to a place where his life was assessed. He was angry that he had to return to "the beaten, diseased hulk" which he felt he had permanently left behind in the hospital. He did not want to return. "Like a spoiled child in a tantrum, I

39

pushed my feet against the wall and fought. There was a sudden sense of hurtling through space. I opened my eyes and looked into the face of a nurse. I had been in a coma for more than two weeks." [5]

A dream of Edgar Sanford is told by his wife, Agnes Sanford, and also by his son John Sanford. In his dream he saw his life in flashback and then watched his body get up and walk out on a path of light into the garden. It brought peace after a period of anxiety and tension.

St. Theresa of the Little Flowers, who died when she was only 22, had the same kind of dream-vision, which brought her serenity and confidence in the last years of her life.

It also appears that this was the experience of Stephen when he was stoned, as recorded in Acts 7.

One day three people came to my office to talk about experiences like these. In nearly every group to whom I lecture I find someone who has had, or heard about, such an experience of penetrating through to learn something of the nature of life after death and then coming back to tell of it.

Experiences of the Departed and of Other Realities

Physical death brings our lives to a rather abrupt and final end from the point of view of ordinary perception. Yet among people in all times there have been consistent reports of some continued relationship with those who have died, reports which say that a person's personality does not decompose like his body. Among many primitive peoples the belief in an afterlife is evident in a fear of ghosts and spirits of the dead, against which one needs protection. In whatever form, nearly all people have had some idea of life persisting after death in spite of the lack of ordinary sensory data. I have sometimes wondered if the express disbelief in life after death which seems to come with a materialistic view of the world may not be an unconscious cop-out because people fear the responsibility of continued existence.

As we consider these extrasensory perceptions, we are stepping into an area where sensory functions cannot reach, and so we have no material data to confirm what is perceived. The best we can do is to try to understand why there is no good reason to *disbelieve* in life after death, and then to look at the evidence which has been collected and consider it as carefully and critically as possible.

One of the most comprehensive and thoughtful theories relating to this question is offered by Lawrence LeShan as an appendix to his book *The Medium, the Mystic and the Physicist*. His basic argument is that in the field theory which has shaped the world view of many thinkers since Einstein, the words *time, create, cease to exist* lose their meaning. He suggests that consciousness continues at the peak level which it has reached before death, and that the religious and mystical way brings one to a state where meaningful survival is possible. The fact that the psyche has experiences that transcend space and time in itself suggests that this core of our being is not totally tied to physical, space-time existence.

Two researchers working with the problem of suicide in Los Angeles were amazed at how often, in the course of their interviews, people who showed suicidal tendencies referred to contact with the dead. They searched the literature of various disciplines in vain for any survey of the belief patterns of human beings in regard to life after death.

The students then got a grant from the National Insti-

41

tute of Mental Health to conduct their own survey, and they did a very careful job. Their results were published in the *Journal for the Scientific Study of Religion* of June-July 1973. Four different racial groups were studied, and the questions were phrased to eliminate any possibility of an interviewer revealing scorn or disbelief and failing to come back with straight answers. The results were startling. Not only was the rate of belief in life after death high, but there was no particular difference between racial, cultural, or educational backgrounds. More than 40 percent of the people reported some experience of contact with one or more individuals who had died. Often the experience had occurred in a dream.

People who are approaching death themselves seem to be particularly open to experiences of others who have died. A study by Karlis Osis included a question about these experiences.[6] He surveyed ten thousand doctors and nurses, selected at random, asking about the experiences of dying patients, their moods, and any visions they had of the dead. The answers reported 1370 such visionary encounters seen by terminal patients. These experiences appear to occur about ten times more often among the dying than among people in normal health. One possible explanation is that those about to step over through death are met by someone already on the other side.

Aside from the work of the Psychical Research societies, these surveys almost exhaust the efforts at serious research in this area. They do show, however, that people continue to have experiences similar to those described in religious literature, like Samuel's rising before Saul (1 Samuel 28). In later times St. Ambrose of Milan wrote of a continued relationship with his deceased brother Satyrus through his dreams. Sulpitius Severus described how he saw St. Martin of Tours taken up into the heavens almost at the moment of his death and before the news could possibly have come in the ordinary way.

For years I have collected such accounts, and everywhere I go there seems to be someone who wants to share such an experience. Often these experiences happen over great distances. A friend was very fond of her mother-in-law, who was sick in another part of the country. They were eagerly preparing for her arrival to finish recuperating in their home. Early one morning my friend awoke to see two angels standing just within the room, and in a moment her mother-in-law appeared at the window and was embraced by the angels. She looked joyous, and in her familiar voice said, "I've finally made it!" Then they glided away, almost close enough to touch. The woman was thinking about waking her husband to tell him how well his mother looked and what a glowing experience of joy filled the room. Instead the telephone awakened him, and he answered it to hear the news that his mother had just died.

The subject of ghosts and haunting is another matter. While the belief in them is found almost all over the world, and some places seem to be the particular haunts of ghosts, over the years these experiences have attracted mostly storytellers and those interested in folklore. The suggestion is made, however, by students as diverse as Dante, Jung, LeShan, and Ford that ghosts may be those mortals who were so attached to the physical world that they are unable to separate from it. They often seem to be dull and uninteresting characters, and perhaps this explains why so many of the personalities dredged up by mediums are so colorless.

In most religions there is also a belief that other kinds of beings can come into contact with humans in various ways. For instance, elaborate hierarchies of gods and goddesses and other beings are found in Greek, Roman, Hindu, and Chinese thought, as well as in most other religious groups. There are many descriptions of angelic beings in the Bible. Beginning with Abraham, angels were understood as the messengers of God, and they are found in story after story. Isaiah, for instance, in his vision saw the seraphim surrounding the Lord on his throne. Paul even spoke of different levels of angels.

Demons were apparently not seen and described until a later time. But they could be heard and spoken with, and their role in causing human problems, particularly mental and physical illness, is presented in the New Testament. I have written a short account of these entities in the New Testament entitled, *The Reality of the Spiritual World*.

The same belief continued through the Middle Ages. The great Thomas Aquinas was called the "angelic doctor," not because of his virtue, but because of his discussions of the angelic nature. In modern times, however, these experiences have been repressed except for an occasional vision like the one I have just described in connection with a death. For religion that sees the world through materialistic eyes, as Bultmann and Bishop Robinson see it, such beings are an absurdity.

The only serious modern study of the subject is by C. G. Jung who sees the experiences of encountering angels or demons as confrontations with power centers (perhaps even with a personality and will of their own). For modern comfort he has renamed these forces archetypes. They appear to be autonomous forces operating from beyond the human personality that can affect human beings and their actions and reactions, and can even have effects on the physical world directly.[7] Carlos Castaneda has described the "allies" he encountered in various experiences in much the same way.

Psychokinesis

The next group of experiences may seem even harder for us to accept today. But once it is established that the human mind can communicate through telepathy, it is no big jump to believe that the mind can influence supposedly inert physical matter. In order to become known, telepathic communication has to affect the physical matter in the brain. It makes little difference whether the communication influences another brain or influences another psyche which then activates another brain. Mind seems to have power over matter.

One reason we have difficulty accepting psychokinesis is that we forget that matter is not as solid and substantial as it appears. As Lyall Watson points out, matter consists of atoms which are mostly electrical fields, and if we could blow an atom up to the size of an Olympic stadium, the actual core of matter in it would be about the size of a pea. The rest is space, empty except for charged particles so small they are hard to imagine. While it is hard to think about a mind having much effect on a tight package of atoms like solid billiard balls, the reality of all the open space makes it easier to imagine that such psychic influence is possible.

The belief that some individuals have power over inert things has been around for a long time. Crapshooters have often believed that they could make certain numbers come up on the dice more frequently than others. In fact it was a young gambler who got down on the floor of J. B. Rhine's office at Duke University and showed the scientist enough to start the first serious investigation of psychokinetic influences. Some of the first tests produced results that could happen by chance only once in more than a billion times.[8] But Dr. Rhine wanted to be as certain as possible. The tests continued over the years with refined techniques and tighter controls, and continued results. Rhine finally concluded that there is so much evidence of direct mental or psychic effect on matter that "merely to repeat PK [psychokinetic] tests with the simple objective of finding more evidence of the PK effect should be an unthinkable waste of time." [9]

One of the most difficult later tests was undertaken at the Utomskii Institute in Leningrad. Nelya Mikhailova was being studied because of her amazing capacity to produce psychokinetic effects. At the high point a raw egg was broken into an aquarium, and from several feet away she was asked to separate the yolk from the white and move them away from each other. She was wired up to all sorts of instruments. After thirty minutes of intense concentration the egg separated. During this time she had lost two pounds and suffered other temporary effects. The indicators showed intense magnetic and electrostatic activity around her body that extended out about a foot, but none of these currents could have reached the aquarium. "As the scientists concluded, the electromagnetic energy was an indicator, a sort of measurable side effect, of a powerful, mysterious field which was stretching from Nelya to the egg." [10]

At Duke, Dr. Helmut Schmidt later modified his precognitive experiment with strontium 90 in order to test for psychokinetic effects. He reasoned that smaller particles might be manipulated more easily than eggs. He arranged nine lights in a circle, which would be turned on one at a time by the decay of a nucleus. Instead of guessing what part of the strontium would explode next, the subjects were asked to force the release of the beta particles to keep the lights moving as chosen, either clockwise or counterclockwise. Schmidt worked with fifteen individuals, none of whom claimed to have any PK ability. Some of them had no success at all, but those who achieved positive results came out better than 1000 to 1 against chance. Apparently even relatively untalented people can direct the next move of a subatomic particle.

Another type of psychokinesis is being investigated by necessity. This is the uncontrolled and often highly destructive effect known as poltergeist activity. *Poltergeist* means noisy spirit, and it is used today to describe the strange and sudden movement of objects, jumping off of shelves or flying through the air with no known being or force moving them.

Until recently most people dismissed the occurrences as products of overwrought and superstitious imagination. But interest in psi has now led to the study of several clearcut examples of this phenomenon. It seems to be connected, almost without exception, with disturbed teenagers, and the incidents cease as soon as they are removed or become aware of their problems. The researchers have found a consistent pattern in the cases they have studied.

One of the most notable series of incidents occurred in a Miami warehouse filled with bric-a-brac, where the breakages became a serious problem. They happened only during working hours and only when a 19-year-old Cuban refugee was present. Things flew off the shelf when his back was turned and always fell to his left and away from him, and in a declining arc. The boy had suffered severe emotional problems. He was studied by Dr. William G. Roll of the University of Virginia and Dr. J. G. Pratt of Duke University, who found, for one thing, that he generally felt release of tension when an incident occurred. His emotional life has now become stabilized, and he no longer causes such incidents.

Wondering about these unconscious poltergeist reactions made one scientist, James Davis, ask himself if other forms of life might produce PK effects as well as teenagers. His first work was with baby chicks who still needed constant warmth to stay alive. He put them under a light hooked up to a random generator set to stay on for only 12 hours. Although it functioned perfectly when the chicks were not there, somehow they managed to keep the light on longer than it was programmed to stay on. The same experiment was then tried with eggs just seven days from hatching, with hard-boiled eggs as a control group. Again the generator functioned perfectly when hard-boiled eggs were under the light. And again, for the incubating eggs it kept coming on more than it should, so that they hatched. Unconscious life forces seem able to direct mechanical equipment for self-preservation.

There are many interesting variations on these PK effects. For example, Ted Serios seems able to project his mental images onto photographic negatives. The results have appeared under conditions controlled as carefully as possible.

Konstantin Raudive, it appears, can do something of this sort to electromagnetic tape, producing voices on it which speak in the seven different languages he knows, although under control he is heard to speak in only one language.

Biofeedback appears to be still another variation of psychokinesis, and one with amazingly practical uses. Doctors have discovered that certain physiological functions which were thought to be simply automatic can be controlled voluntarily if a patient is given repeated signals when the desired level of functioning is reached. Patients have learned to lower their high blood pressure, to produce alpha waves in the brain, to relax muscle spasms or even to control gastric juices, as Dr. Barbara Brown shows in her fascinating book, *New Mind, New Body*. This control is not achieved through any known route in the nervous system. It appears rather that the psyche influences the organ or tissues directly. There is not so much a "learned" response, but a psychokinetic effect on functions otherwise beyond our reach. In some ways biofeedback effects resemble the amazing control of bodily processes that can come through the practice of yoga, even to the ability to walk over red hot coals without being burned.

Religious and Psychic Healing

One more of these strange psychic abilities can also have direct effects on the human body—healing which has been associated with religious practice in nearly all cultures. Besides shrines and rituals which can transmit a remarkable healing effect, certain people are especially gifted or can be trained to have this effect. Among them are shamans and witchdoctors, who may use various objects to produce healing, as well as Christian healers and others who were generally frowned upon by medical science early in this century.

Since then, however, many scientists have come to see the reality of these influences on people's state of health or illness. For instance, a feature article in *The New York Times* of July 7, 1972, carefully described the support being given by the National Institute of Mental Health to maintain the training of shamans among the Navajo Indians in Arizona and New Mexico. Impartial observers have gone to the spot to see what happens and have witnessed healings by medicine men when the local hospitals and medical science were unable to help the patient.

One group of physicians and psychologists have joined together to sponsor two recent conferences on psychic healing. The reports of their findings and the discussions have been published in two excellent books, *The Varieties of Healing Experience: Exploring Psychic Phenomena in Healing* and *The Dimensions of Healing: A Symposium.*[11] Both volumes offer interesting reports on many aspects of

49

parapsychological healing. Another excellent theoretical treatment of healing is found in LeShan's *The Medium, the Mystic and the Physicist.*

One of these reports is on acupuncture which appears to operate through psi channels rather than through ordinary physical ones, and which works so well that Western doctors are beginning to investigate it.

Kirlian photography is another area being studied. This new lensless electrical photography, developed in Russia, reveals "auras" or fields of something similar to energy radiating around living things. It has been used to show changes in the hands of both a healer and the patient resulting from the act of laying on of hands. The photographs show a marked decrease in the aura around the healer's fingers after the experience and an even more striking increase in the "radiation" around the patient's fingers. No one knows for sure what this means, but it is certain that something has occurred and that it can be pictured.

A number of experiments have tested the effectiveness of healers. The most dramatic of them is the work of Sister Justa Smith at Rosary Hill College in Buffalo. She worked with a well-known healer, Colonel Oskar Estebany, whose effect on injured mice had already been studied successfully by Dr. Bernard Grad at McGill University in Montreal. In these tests a carefully measured strip of fur and skin was cut from the flank of each mouse, leaving an exposed wound. One group was then treated by Colonel Estebany by laying on of hands, while the rest were left to recover by ordinary bodily processes. The cages were handled with strict controls to eliminate any other influence or interference. The mice treated by laying on of hands recovered at a far faster rate than those left alone. In the new experiments it was shown that this healer had a marked effect in increasing the activity of the enzyme trypsin, both in a normal state and after it had been damaged by ultraviolet irradiation. Since the enzyme was in a test tube and not in someone's body, no one could claim that it was just reacting to suggestion!

Dr. Grad and others have made similar tests of the ability of healers to influence plant growth with equally impressive results. Certain people apparently have a healing touch which can help animals, plants, and enzymes, and also human beings.

Dolores Krieger, professor of nursing at New York University, recently tested the healing touch among the nurses with whom she works. A number of nurses were trained and used the healing touch with the patients under their care. An objective test was then used to compare these patients with the control group who were cared for in the ordinary way. The hemoglobin of both groups was checked, and it was found to be significantly higher in the patients cared for with the healing touch. Dr. Krieger has described this experiment in an article entitled "Therapeutic Touch: The Imprimatur of Nursing," in the May 1975 issue of the *American Journal of Nursing.* It is unfortunate that she apparently did not realize that such a tradition of healing exists in Christianity, and she based her experiment on the instructions of Eastern religion.

In my book *Healing and Christianity* I have traced the close connection between Christian practice and healing, which is still found wherever a church has been able to avoid the negative ideas of the Enlightenment and its totally materialistic framework. I have also tried to give an understanding of the changing attitude of modern medicine and how physicians have come to realize that intangible things like emotions, faith, and confidence have a very direct effect upon the human body.

51

When one cannot handle them, the emotions of fear and anxiety, anger and hostility, depression and psychic pain can be as destructive as a dose of poison. Yet how can these emotions be controlled? How can we avoid being fearful and anxious if we find ourselves in an indifferent or even hostile world with only the extinction of the grave in the end?

The answer of some people is to turn on other human beings with anger and hatred and let loose their resentment for being trapped in a meaningless world with no exit but death. But many people respond to this prospect by depression and the torment of inner agony. With depression so common today that it is called the "common cold of psychiatry," there is a growing realization that unless people can find some way to handle these feelings, they become a means of self-destruction. The body itself begins to take the fear and tension and ends up reacting on its own.

If there is any way to break the cycle of meaninglessness and the emotions it arouses, it is to find some center of meaning, some value and concern rooted in the very substance of the universe. There is then a possibility of change, and in this process we can see the bridge from religion to the body, from the religious to the moral to the psychological, and then to the physical. Since emotions usually strike with sickness when we are the most unconscious, both medicine and the church need individuals who are trained to recognize these symptoms and are able to work together to bring meaning and health to these individuals.

Physicians have begun to realize that the body is a delicate balance of energies responding to all sorts of forces that cannot be picked up by ordinary sense experience and reacting in ways that cannot be dealt with by physical methods alone. Dr. Jerome Frank, a Johns Hopkins professor of psychiatry, writes that faith is as effective in healing some diseases as penicillin is in treating others.[12]

Dr. Christiaan Barnard has realized somewhat the same thing. He was once asked about his arthritis and the difficulty of doing heart transplants, and he replied that he had recovered. Then he went on to say that arthritis is an allergy like hay fever, and that a cure for it would probably be found when physicians had discovered how to keep organ transplants from being rejected. He told how lymphocytes, those tiny white blood cells that destroy bacteria, get too active and turn on the body itself, often attacking the connective tissue of the joints. Probably, Dr. Barnard suggested, the reason for arthritis is that the person hates himself.

Much of this medical evidence is found in my book on healing. But the importance of the lymphocytes and their relation to emotion and stress was only partly understood when that book was written. It was known then that if a throat culture, for instance, were taken from everyone who reads this page, every one of them would show a few streptococci. Why don't these bacteria take over and knock us down with a strep throat? Without our knowing it, the lymphocytes attack the bacteria. Then more lymphocytes are produced. But if the body is overtired or is suffering psychological or emotional stress, this army of tiny corpuscles fails and the person becomes sick.

Now it has been discovered that repelling cancer cells is also a responsibility of the lymphocytes. One can actually see the fight against cancer take place, magnified onto a movie screen. This breakthrough film—in lapsed time and magnified 3000 times—was produced by the American Cancer Society and is entitled, *The Embattled Cell*. It shows living lung tissue with colonies of cancer cells being attacked and destroyed by lymphocytes. It reveals the kind of purposeful activity going on in one small part of the body. Anyone who thinks of the body as a simple, physical mechanism will find this film most illuminating. Inside we are more like a teeming city, bustling day and night. And it does not take much imagination on our part to realize how this purposeful energy can be either channeled towards healing, or misdirected to self-destruction by emotions like anger or fear or despair. This current work on lymphocytes opens up questions we cannot afford to avoid.

No religion has been more concerned with opening channels of healing than the Christianity of the New Testament and the early church. This is a truly guiding principle of the Christian tradition. And the practice of it by sacramental and religious means is certainly closer to psi than to physical medicine. This religious practice speaks of a human body and a physical world far more sensitive to spiritual and mental influences than most modern theologians have envisioned. The things ESP researchers have been proving offer us Christians a key to the meaning of healing for our churches and for our own lives.

A Perspective

In this brief sketch of the highlights in ESP research, it is apparent that the mass of information being gathered makes it difficult to deny that these things happen. Indeed, trying to shut out the flood of new data is like building a sand wall against a rising tide. Those who deny extrasensory perception and the effect of mind and psyche upon physical objects and in healing simply do not know the world in which they are living. Neither do they have a grasp of religious practice and its connection with healing in all parts of the world. The facts are being shown, whatever rationalistic theologians think about them.

54

But what are we to do with these facts? Are psychic phenomena tainted and somehow evil, or are they simply neutral human capacities that may be used for good or evil? To find the answers, we need to know how these experiences happen to come to people. Let's look now at the ways we experience psi phenomena.

3

How We
Experience ESP

Early psychological researchers who studied how we perceive through the senses learned much about the physiology of sensation. They were interested in how light waves or sound waves, an object one touched, or the action of a chemical can set off electrical charges in nerve tissue so that something travels to the brain and becomes sensation.

Today, as more data accumulates about non-sensory experience, people have become interested in how we are able to participate in experiences of ESP. Students want to know about altered states of consciousness (or ASCs for short), and they turn to one of the best studies, Charles Tart's *Altered States of Consciousness.*

It is possible to distinguish six different ways through which we arrive at an altered state of consciousness, all of them ways in which we share in psi events.

First, there is the natural ASC of *dreaming* in which these experiences usually occur without any effort on the part of the percipient. Dreams are given. They come to everyone four to six times every night. Of course, one must learn to remember them, but we have little to do with creating them. Visions and intuitions are a similar way in which psi experiences can become known during waking consciousness.

A second way of stepping into an altered state of consciousness is through *meditation* and *religious ritual*. In meditating a person makes a purposeful and willed effort to reach a different level of awareness, while religious rituals sometimes open a door so that a worshiper is led by the images and symbols into another reality. In either case it is quite possible for healing or prophetic (precognitive) or any other of these experiences to occur.

A third way is a *trance,* in which one loses consciousness and apparently becomes a mouthpiece for realities operating from a nonphysical plane. Some people find this experience, to a lesser degree, by using instruments like an ouija board or by attempting automatic writing.

In the fourth method, *hypnotic trance,* one steps into an altered state of consciousness through the agency and suggestion of another person.

The fifth method of using *hallucinogenic drugs* can also induce an alteration of consciousness.

Finally there is an *indirect way* of making contact with another reality. By consulting an oracle, seeking an omen, or conferring with someone skilled in relationship with the other realm, a person may tap the data or the results available, usually without stepping over into altered consciousness.

Any of these methods can open different individuals to various experiences of the kind I have described. Some of these ways of altering consciousness seem more natural and less dangerous than others. All of them seem to indicate that there is another level of reality which one can experience. This realm is real, and many people believe there is need to deal with these realities. Let us look at each of these methods more closely.

1. Dreams and ESP

Until William Dement opened the door to the physiological study of dreams in the 1950s, not even the psychologists persuaded many people to take dreams seriously.[1] Before this time most people believed such an idea was for superstitious people who believed in old wives' tales.

Now that it is possible to know when a person is dreaming, one can be awakened to tell about the contents of a dream. Dreaming periods, we are now very sure, happen to everyone at least four times a night; they last from a few minutes to an hour or more; and they can be pinned down by various physiological changes. Two of these changes are relatively easy to spot. First there is rapid eye movement during vivid dreaming, which gives these periods the name REM sleep. And second, there is a definite change in brain waves, and the brain waves can be recorded on an electroencephalograph.

Some people, of course, have always believed that dreams give clairvoyant, telepathic, and precognitive information. But this could be laughed off as mere coincidences until the work of Montague Ullman, Stanley Krippner, and Charles Honorton. Using the new laboratory methods of pinpointing dreams, they have shown that such information does get through in dreams. And what is more important, given the right conditions, these experiences can happen to many people. This work was begun because Dr. Ullman could not forget one patient's dream which revealed intimate details about the physician's life only he could have known. The experiments, which have been described in two books, were carried out with tight controls so that no accusation of fraud could be leveled.[2]

One of the most important implications of this work is

that it confirms the studies of various depth psychologists who believe that dreams are windows into another reality. Finding that a dream has brought knowledge about the physical world which did not — or could not — come through the senses is an eye opener. Then one is likely to pay attention to the idea that dreams offer contact with nonphysical reality—call it either psychic or spiritual. One may then be open to looking into some of Jung's twenty volumes that give us a view of ourselves and our world quite different from the idea of materialistic science of the early 1900s. Dreams gave Jung his most significant insights into the nature of the nonphysical world.

Besides giving ESP information about the world of space-time experience, with occasionally even a clue that guides scientific discovery, dreams reveal a whole range of nonphysical reality.[3] Most people believe that they provide insights into our own unconscious attitudes, and that they can bring up forgotten incidents out of our past. In addition, they also seem to give information about the innate structure of the psyche, revealing things that are common to all men everywhere, as cross-cultural studies show. But this is not all.

There is another area far more significant for our lives which dreams show us. It is a whole realm of reality which is like the individual's psyche but separated from it. This realm Jung has called the collective unconscious or objective psyche, and in other places he suggested that the realities in it have a psychoid, or more than only psychic, base. The descriptions of this realm seem to fit what most non-Western peoples have called spiritual reality. In this reality one finds an organizing force or principle, which appears to be the same principle, in fact, that gives us the dream itself and which is wise enough to compensate for our one-sided ego attitudes. It is called "the dreamer within" by Dr. Alan McGlashan in his penetrating book *The Savage and the Beautiful Country.* He suggests that there is a close relationship between "the dreamer within" and the creative, guiding spirit which Christians have called the Holy Spirit.

One meets more than just memories in dreams. Persons themselves, alive or dead, seem to appear and be met there. Sometimes there are destructive experiences which make one wish that he never had to dream again. In these experiences the negative powers do not hide their destructiveness. While they sometimes seem to be directed by a destructive force or principle, many of them are apparently not so organized, and may even become some of our most constructive experiences when they are faced and dealt with.

Then there are encounters with what appear to be angelic powers that are purely creative and helpful, and here one needs to use real care. The angelic may be real, but the most dangerous appearance of evil is the one that appears to be an angel of light. In addition, one meets entities that are both good and evil. These forces seem to be innate patterns of energy, or bundles of psychoid power, to which Jung gives the name "archetypes."

Sometimes there are clear dreams in which it appears that God or the Spirit speaks to our questions directly and with clarity.

And finally there are experiences in which one is given an overview of reality, or is ushered into the very presence of God, where one seems to meet him face to face, and the whole of one's life is thus given solid meaning.

I have kept careful record of my dreams for nearly 30 years and have found most of these levels in my own experience. I have also found them described in the New Testament and in the writings of the church fathers.

Visions break through into ordinary consciousness in the same way that dreams are given in sleep, and many

61

more people have visions than is generally known.[4] But the materialistic attitude in Western culture keeps most people from speaking to others about visions or any of their other mystical experiences. People are afraid of being laughed at or considered strange. Sometimes people fear they are hallucinating.

There is a difference between hallucinations and visions, however. In either one we can, and often do, come into contact with contents from deep within our psyches. The individual who is hallucinating believes these contents come from the outside world. For example, he sees his dragons and his angels, whatever person or thing they look like, coming at him down the street. People who have a vision or a dream know that they have seen something from within or from somewhere besides the physical world. They may or may not know that it comes from another realm of reality, but if they do, they realize that it is real to them in a different sense from what is real in the physical world. We hallucinate only when we get the two realms (the inner and the outer) mixed up. One of the tasks of childhood is learning to distinguish between these two realms.

Hebrew and Greek, the original languages of the Bible, make almost no distinction between dreams and visions. The words for "dreams" and "visions" in these languages clearly show an understanding that people have experiences of two different kinds of reality. In my book on dreams I have identified 12 ways in which New Testament writers described their contacts with another world. Modern researchers would call these contacts with another world or realm *psi experiences*. At least one of these ways includes the idea of intuitions, which appear to be mental insights or revelations in which problems are solved or insights are revealed to us in much the same way that visions are given. The idea or insight comes to us without our asking and without our cooperation.

One cannot produce these dream or vision experiences if they will not come. They seem to be autonomous. One can learn to listen to the dreams that do come, and follow a number of valuable suggestions that will help in doing this. Panati gives an excellent list at the end of his chapter on dreams in *Supersenses*. In these ways, and also by developing imagination, one may find help in becoming more open to these experiences. But on the whole dreams and visions and intuitions are just given. Through meditation, however, one can help imagination along.

2. Meditation and Religious Ritual

I have been pondering the subject of meditation for many years, and have finally put the ideas that developed into a book—*The Other Side of Silence: A Guide to Christian Meditation.* I have come to the conclusion that meditation is any process that can help one develop a new state of consciousness and a personal experience of coming into relationship with the divine. This is a complex process which may be described in various ways.

There are basically three different kinds of meditation. There is first the practice frequently found in the East and among some mystics in the West, in which one withdraws from the ordinary sensory world and is slowly absorbed into the cosmic mind. This destination or state of consciousness is indefinable since, if the effort is successful, the ego is lost and no longer exists.

A second kind is classical Christian meditation. In this practice one seeks quiet in order to come into an inner world and there to bring the totality of one's being into contact with another reality, the reality of the Christ.

Visions and images continue to be important, and they are not seen as just a way for beginners or for those who can't come to a full relationship with this other reality. The effort is to bring one's whole being to a different state of consciousness, and not to lose any part of it.

The third kind of meditation is found in religious services in which one acts out or chants or dances a ritual connected with history, usually in a sacred place or in the presence of sacred objects. This kind of sacramental meditation opens up experiences of another reality, a divine reality, and it is just as real as any other way of letting down the conscious barriers.

What is important from the Christian point of view is not *how* one arrives at these experiences, but whether they are deep and real enough to allow the love from God to flow into the individual and then allow that individual to express this love and concern outwardly towards other human beings.

Religious experience which has this result is the goal of Christian meditation. Probably the most profound and careful study of it was made by Baron von Hügel in *The Mystical Element of Religion*. He makes the point that when human beings exalt the mystical element, to the neglect of the historical and intellectual, then religious life and practice get off the track. I concur heartily. We need to withdraw from sensory experience and touch as much of the center of things as can be found, but not to be absorbed by such immediate experiences of the divine. We also need the historical approach and all our critical faculties if we are to know and use the experiences to their fullest.

Several experiments have been made relating to meditation. Some of the most interesting of them use techniques to help individuals reach a state of consciousness that brings contact with the nonphysical world. One is the method known as sensory deprivation, while the other is a technique for fixing a person's attention in a way that seems to produce a state of consciousness similar to that attained through yoga, or by using a mantra in Transcendental Meditation, or by the practice of the Jesus prayer or the chant of the Hare Krishna people.

The latter method uses a device that produces a completely fixed image on the retina of the eye. A tiny projector is mounted on a contact lens, and when it is fixed in place, the image falls in exactly the same spot no matter how much the person shifts his eyes. The image quickly disappears from sight and alpha brain waves—which are known to be the basic pattern in the meditative state—begin to appear.[5] While the reports of this work do not specify what happens on the visual screen after that, it is likely that spontaneous images also begin to appear. When attention is totally fixed on some object or sound, a person seems to move naturally into an altered state of consciousness and contact with some kind of non-sensory perception.

This is usually the experience of people who are placed in a sensory deprivation chamber, cut off from external stimuli as completely as possible. Dr. Woodburn Heron of McGill University has written about the psycho-physical aspects of sensory deprivation. He placed individuals in a bath of water at constant body temperature and eliminated all sensation possible. He discovered that a regular pattern developed. First the person experienced blackness, then simple visions, and finally full-fledged imaginative fantasies. As other researchers have noted, the alpha waves characteristic of meditation go along with this. Some subjects after hours of deprivation received telepathic impressions from distant friends. Others had clairvoyant visions of things that were actually happening in other parts of the laboratory. Many of the researchers and subjects developed an intense interest in parapsychology and read everything they could find on the subject.

In a religious service where the environment is fixed in a familiar pattern, including music or chanting and a feeling of closeness to the people present, a person sometimes lets down the barriers and steps into an experience of another realm of reality. Being open to suggestion, of course, can help such an experience occur. What appears to happen is that the person enters a new level of being and consciousness where the figures of the myth and the ritual appear and speak. This can be a genuine religious encounter, and also one that rates high in safety. Most religious rituals have been tested over the years and have many built-in safeguards. The fact that there is also a group with whom to relate helps a person keep one foot in the material world while living out such an experience.

Most meditation which brings one into contact with another realm of being, however, is done alone. One faces another reality, whether it is seen as images or felt as sinking into the cosmic mind, and there are dangers. An individual can become so absorbed in the images that arise from the other realm that he loses contact or interest in ordinary things. Zen recognizes this danger very clearly. Getting lost in *makyo* or "the world of the devil" where images take over, is a common experience known to Japanese doctors as "Zen madness."

There are dangers even in so tame a form of meditation as that suggested for businessmen by Dr. Herbert Benson in the *Harvard Business Review* of July-August 1974. His article, "Your Innate Asset for Combating Stress," describes a technique of relaxation while repeating some one-syllable word quietly, to be practiced for twenty minutes twice a day. Probably not many people are disciplined enough to keep at either TM or this demystified form of it to the point of hurting themselves. Any form of meditation requires more force of will than taking a pill or smoking marijuana. Still, Dr. Benson realizes that it has very positive effects, and that there are those who feel that if some is good, more must be better. He cautions that trying the technique for long periods can have strange effects, and that some individuals may even suffer disorientation.

Another danger in practicing meditation is the possibility of becoming so intent on imageless union with the center of being that one is cut off from his own emotional life. If one does not keep working away at emotional problems, the unconscious can explode in reaction and play havoc. To keep things in balance we often need fellowship and guidance on this path of meditation.

Clairvoyance, telepathy, and healing abilities are often found among those who are adept in meditation. These people seem to step back and forth between this world and another state of consciousness, or a realm where space and time do not hold rigidly.

Many healers speak of the necessity of reaching some such state through meditation. Agnes Sanford tells how effective it is to imagine a sick person radiantly well with a healing light flooding through them. I have seen similar results by coming into touch with Christ in meditation and then, in visual images, bringing the sick person into his presence to be touched by him. On the other hand, if one is anxious or distraught and tries to heal, the effect seems to be impeded.

This approach to visual images is one of the main differences between the way of the East and the kind of meditation found in early Christianity. Instead of seeking an experience of union, the early Christians consciously tried to relate to the realm from which dreams and visions come. In this kind of meditation one does not push the inner images aside. The effort is to work with them in order to stay open to this other reality, and the same kind of paranormal experiences can happen as occur in dreams.

Common in the early church and among pentecostal Christians today is the belief that people can become open to the action of the Holy Spirit. For some groups the evidence that the Spirit is present is the experience of tongue speaking, which is certainly an expression of the deep unconscious and related to parapsychological capacities. Psychologically, tongue speaking might be called a motor vision. The brain centers connected with speech are activated, rather than the visual and auditory centers that produce visions. Along with this often goes the gift of prophecy in which the message pours out spontaneously, but in the speaker's own language. In addition, when these religious expressions occur, experiences of clairvoyance, telepathy, precognition, and healing frequently seem to follow, and these experiences are generally attributed to the action of the Holy Spirit. Although these groups are often criticized on psychological grounds, there seems to be little evidence of psychological danger in this religious expression, as I have pointed out in my book *Tongue Speaking*.

3. Trances, Mediums, Ouija Boards, and Automatic Writing

Thus far we have been discussing states of consciousness in which ESP experiences are found, but in which these experiences are essentially a by-product. Dreams come when we are trying to get some rest, and if we pay attention to them, it is usually so that we may find meaning and direction in our lives, not ESP experiences. In religious rituals and meditation, and also in tongue speaking and prophecy, one is seeking relationship of one kind or another with the center of spiritual reality. Even the idea of being given such a capacity as healing comes later. One is seeking the giver and not the gifts.

There is a different emphasis in mediumship and trances. These altered states of consciousness are also mostly given, but the concern with them is to produce the ESP experiences themselves. A medium goes into a trance to use her controlled experience to contact some deceased person or to obtain ESP information, or sometimes to bring healing. There may, or may not, be a religious attitude. Often the practice itself becomes a religion.

Fraud is a real danger when people who are bereaved go to mediums. There are so-called mediums who simply seek profit from people who are lost and confused, and apparently some people are simple and suggestive enough to accept what they say as fact. Yet in spite of such frauds and the damage they do, there seem to be mediums who are actually in touch with another reality and offer genuine information. In *The Life Beyond Death* Arthur Ford tells some of the recent history of serious psychics and how they have used very sophisticated research tools in attempting to show that the dead are alive and do make contact with the living.

The late Bishop Pike, certainly a skeptical soul, wrote in *The Other Side* about his experiences with both Ford and a well-known British psychic, but he also warned about seeking these experiences for their own sake. Diane Pike tells how the same British psychic also helped her locate her husband's body where he had finally wandered in the Dead Sea desert.

Jung investigated this kind of phenomena. He came to the conclusion that some real hints are given about life after death, but he went on to say that "too much traffic with these germs of myth is dangerous for weak and suggestible minds, for they are led to mistake vague intimations for substantial knowledge, and to hypostatize mere phantasms."[6] Human wish-fulfillment can distort such materials, or some people can become so involved with these concerns that they lose contact with ordinary life.

Edgar Cayce, who was unlettered but deeply sincere, was one of the greatest psychics. For nearly 40 years he helped people with medical problems by going into a trance each day and saying out loud what came to him unconsciously. With only the names of the sick persons and where they lived, he would apparently make psychic contact with each of them, diagnose the disease, and prescribe for it. His rate of correct diagnosis and healing was phenomenal. Stenographic reports of thirty years of his trance utterances are on file at the Association for Research and Enlightenment in Virginia Beach, Virginia. There are two excellent summaries of his life, *Venture Inward* by his son, Hugh Lynn Cayce, and *There Is a River* by Thomas Sugrue.

Thousands of people have been attracted to Edgar Cayce groups all over the country who are looking for religious teaching not subservient to materialism. Whether or not one accepts Cayce's teachings on reincarnation and life-readings, he is a person and a phenomenon to be reckoned with. He made it a rule never to take money for his work, and the few times he was persuaded to use his powers for gain, he lost them. He was a faithful member of a Christian church and taught an adult Bible class in an orthodox way until his death. Those interested in Cayce have been largely responsible for organizing the Academy of Parapsychology and Medicine.

A team connected with this group have also investigated the Brazilian psychic, Arigo, and the amazing reports of his going into a trance and doing successful surgery with a rusty knife. They were deeply impressed by his powers, and brought back pictures of his surgery. This story is told by John Fuller in *Arigo: Surgeon of the Rusty Knife.*

Others could also be mentioned, people like Eileen Garrett with great and genuine powers. These phenomena have occurred throughout history and have left a deep imprint on our traditions and on our real beliefs which pop out whenever something pierces the rationalistic crust. Many of us are beginning to realize that in these psychic individuals something of importance surfaces, which needs to be studied and understood.

In addition to professional mediums, reputable and not so reputable, individuals sometimes try invoking some spirit or other on their own. This is a dangerous undertaking, because now and then it succeeds. I learned of one such experience the day I was asked to speak to children in a religion class in South Bend. I was trying to explain the possibility of another world beside the physical, when several of them began to talk excitedly. They knew what I meant, and they told me about the evening when a group of them had decided to have a séance. They lit a candle in an upstairs room, put a picture of Bobby Kennedy on the table and began to chant, "Come, Bobby, come." And, they told me in horror, something came. A girl downstairs fainted. Séances are not to be played with. There is a realm which can be contacted, but is not always pleasant or creative to deal with.

Another way of coming into contact with the realm which mediums reach is by using an ouija board, one of the most popular games in America. It was invented early in the 1900s and named after *oui* in French and *ja* in German. In other words, it is the "yes-yes board." The idea is quite simple. Two people rest their fingers lightly on a small pointer which glides about a board with the alphabet and other signs on it. People who are sensitive to this kind of experience find that they can ask questions of the board and watch the answers being spelled out. Whether the answers come from one's own unconscious or from outside, they often supply amazing insights and even information.

It is unfortunate, however, that so many people make a game of encountering the psychic realm. Instead of dealing with these realities, which are anything but playful, people sometimes toy with them until they get in trouble and have to call for help. This is the background theme expressed in *The Exorcist,* where the action begins to unfold out of the scene of the little girl playing with an ouija board. This device appears to unlock forces few of us today know how to deal with.

Besides using the ouija board people sometimes play with a pendulum in a similar way, holding it above a set of symbols to see how its swing will point out answers to their questions.

Automatic writing is still another way in which psychic forces can emerge and take over part of an individual who is quite conscious and not in a trance. For most of us writing is a very directed and purposeful affair. But people who do automatic writing (sometimes with the help of a planchette which glides easily), have no idea what is coming out until they read it. Some psychic force moves the hand, and a few people even produce lines that have to be held up to a mirror to be read, although they are unable to do this by trying on their own. Automatic writing and also the flow of imagination called "stream of consciousness" writing can both reveal hidden areas of one's personality. Sometimes in such writing a very different and coherent personality emerges, which often brings telepathic and other ESP contacts.

Several interesting books record what came to people in such ways. *The Seth Material* and *Seth Speaks,* in which Jane Roberts writes of the eternal validity of the human soul, are the latest of these. Although some of these writings seem to have been inspired by rather shallow spirits, other such works show true creativity. Many artists, for instance Beethoven and Chopin, have also acknowledged that their inspiration often came from a psychic source.

4. Hypnotic Trance

Hypnotism, which again is quite different from much that we have been discussing, really has to be seen to be believed. On the surface it looks like a simple process. The hypnotist gives a few instructions, sometimes waving some instrument like a pen or simply speaking quietly, and the subject goes into a trance-like state in which his unconscious mind is open to the suggestions given him by the hypnotist. The experience is parapyschological in itself. Under hypnosis surgery can be performed without pain, and before anesthesia it was apparently used by many humane doctors. Many of the effects obtained by biofeedback can be produced through hypnosis. Although it has often been associated more with night club amusement or with mesmerism and animal magnetism, hypnosis is a powerful tool for opening a person up to psi experiences.

Dr. Burton Glick, chief of psychiatric research for New York's Mount Sinai Hospital, had always been most skeptical of ESP phenomena until he read in the *American Journal of Psychiatry* about the work on dream telepathy at Maimonides Hospital. The ideas struck home, and he felt he must test them himself. But he did not have the elaborate equipment for a telepathic experiment, and decided to try testing for clairvoyance under hypnosis.

He worked with a young nurse who was interested and believed that such experiences happen but had shown no ability for them herself. He used the same picture method that Ullman and Krippner had worked out. Several pictures were each wrapped and sealed inside an opaque envelope. A laboratory assistant picked out one of them at random, and when the nurse was deeply hypnotized, Dr. Glick laid the envelope in her lap and instructed her to tell him whatever she thought and felt and imagined about the picture. After a moment she began talking. When the picture—Winslow Homer's *"The Gulf Stream"* —was opened by the independent judges, what was on the tape recorder turned out to be a remarkably accurate description. Somehow she had "seen" inside the envelope. Other experiments have demonstrated similar results.

In other studies one person was hypnotized who then, under suggestion, hypnotized a second subject. Together they entered what seemed to be a common psychic countryside. While under hypnosis they answered questions about what they were experiencing; otherwise they spoke very little. But in the post-hypnotic interviews, each described so much the same experience that it is apparent they were communicating telepathically.

One pair, with whom the experiments were continued over several sessions, also began to share many telepathic experiences outside the laboratory. Ultimately the work had to be broken off for two reasons. The experimenter was finding it harder and harder to bring them out of hypnosis. They did not want to return. In addition, the bond between them had become so close that it was threatening both of their marriages, and by agreement they broke off even their friendship.

In spite of the fact that hypnosis is used so widely and is easy to learn and use, it is not very well understood. Not all people are susceptible to hypnotic trance, but those who are, often find that they have amazing capacities of ESP which they do not have in their ordinary waking state.

There are dangers, however, particularly when hypnotic suggestion is used by someone with questionable ethical standards who finds that it gives power over another person. In addition, it can reveal areas of one's life which the individual may not be able to handle. And when hypnosis is used to remove problems like smoking or biting one's fingernails, other more dangerous problems often move in to take their place. Hypnosis is certainly a valuable research tool, but it should be used with great care and plenty of safeguards.

5. Drugs and ESP

The subject of drug use arouses so much emotion that it is difficult to talk about it objectively, and even harder to hear what is being said. Probably there are two basic reasons why people use drugs. One is to retreat from unpleasant reality and find refuge, even momentarily, in a world that seems less harsh. This use of drugs is a retreat from reality which has much in common with psychosis. One friend who is a psychiatrist refers to alcoholism—and alcohol is as much a drug as heroin—as self-induced psychosis. Another tells his patients that it is all right to drink as long as they don't need it. Unfortunately this rule seldom works with hard drugs. Taking a little drugs is like being a little pregnant. It keeps growing.

The other reason is quite different. Drugs can be used to get into another realm or world and so to widen one's experience of reality or state of consciousness. This use, although potentially dangerous, is not essentially a mechanism of mental illness as much as an effort to experiment with altered states of consciousness. It represents an attempt to expand experience rather than to retreat from reality.

Andrew Weil's *The Natural Mind* is one of the most objective and constructive studies of the drug problem. His thesis is clear-cut and straightforward. Most people using hallucinogenic drugs today are using them because the agencies that once provided relationship with a reality other than the material world have ceased to give this experience. Weil believes that human beings have an innate and instinctive need and desire for altered states of consciousness, and if these are not provided in legitimate ways, they will be found in dangerous and illegal ways. The Roman Empire didn't have much success in three centuries of trying to stamp out Christianity. Weil believes that trying to stamp out drug use by law enforcement will be just as futile.

My experience with college students bears out Weil's contention point by point. Drugs do open the door to altered states of consciousness. When there is no institution of society offering to provide extrasensory experience, men and women will look for such experience outside of those institutions. The task is not to prohibit but to provide healthy ways of experiencing a different kind of consciousness. If the church wants to help the situation, it will make the effort to provide mystical experience, imaginative meditation, and various encounters with more than the physical world which have more to offer the individual than smoking marijuana or popping a pill.

Drugs have been used by many religious groups as part of some ritual to invoke the deity. The Persians used *soma* to become like the gods. Alcohol was used in the Bacchic mysteries. Alice Marriott has made a fascinating study of the religious use of peyote by the Indians in New Mexico, and Carlos Castaneda describes being introduced to peyote and two other drugs by Don Juan, but only as a last resort to detach Castaneda from his materialism. In *The Wizard of the Upper Amazon* Manuel Cordova-Rios and F. Bruce Lamb tell the story of this Spanish youth who was captured by a tribe of the upper Amazon and there initiated, with similar drug rituals and amazing ESP experiences, into the role of medicine man and chief.

As Weil emphasizes, when drugs are used, the use needs

to be surrounded by ritual and contained. Even apart from addiction, if they are taken playfully and without safeguards, they can lead to disaster. LSD, for instance, seems to cause disintegration of the ego structure and, with this, distortion of the person's ordinary perception of the world. Sometimes these effects are irreversible, and they generally occur without warning. Some studies suggest that long use of marijuana leads to a gradual breakdown of ego motives and desires.

The use of drugs, however, is more than just a symptom of revolt. It may be an attempt to provide experiences human beings need. Use of drugs may open individuals to a whole world of psychic reality no one should enter out of idle curiosity, and which many people should not enter at all. If we deny the reality that drugs lead to, we cannot deal creatively with the problem of their use. Young people today find something of the experience they seek in clandestine situations of reaction and revolt, mostly separated from psychic wisdom and stability. It is no wonder they become open in the wrong direction, often with tragic results.

6. Divination or ESP Through Oracles

There is one last way of tapping ESP information that may not open one to an altered state of consciousness at all. This is the use of some kind of oracle as a tool to pry information out of a recalcitrant spiritual or psychic world. When a situation is difficult and human wisdom seems inadequate, many Christians will open the Bible at random and let a pointer pick out some clue about what to do. There are dozens of other ways to test the temper of the times. Many people have considered themselves experts on everything from the livers of sacrificed animals and blemishes on the body to tarot cards, from the flight of birds to tea leaves.[7] Palmistry has been used in the same way. But the recent scientific discovery of characteristic creases in the hands that go with certain specific diseases now tends to make palmistry a medical study.

Two popular methods of divination are astrology and the ancient Chinese book of oracles, the *I Ching* or *Book of Changes.*

In order to understand either one of them, one must put aside the Western idea of causality. There is another point of view which does not look to the *I Ching* or astrology for a direct cause that may determine an event. Instead, the position of the stars in astrology and throwing the coins or the sticks to consult the *I Ching* are seen as ways of finding clues to the inner meaning of the whole cosmos or the entire world at that moment. According to this point of view, there is a spiritual meaning that pervades the entire universe, and the position of the stars and the hexagrams picked out by the coins or sticks also reflect that meaning. Thus they can help to answer the question: What are the conditions that affect a situation?

A person asks the question either to avoid certain possibilities, or to take advantage of certain of them. The answers in both cases provide only potentialities, as do the precognitive suggestions in dreams. This ties in with a theory in Chinese thought that there are fluctuations in the quality of spiritual or psychic nature and that it is important to learn the direction this cycle is taking.

Astrology is a study that has occupied some of the best minds in history, including Thomas Aquinas. We now know that the sun and moon do affect conditions on earth, and that life is astonishingly sensitive to the variations. While we cannot trace much direct effect from the planets and stars, as Lyall Watson shows, there is interesting evidence of wisdom hidden within astrology. Objective experiments have shown that astrologers can study a list of names, simply with each person's birth date, and determine with amazing success which individuals have a certain characteristic and which of them do not have it. Undoubtedly they use not only their fixed methods, but also use intuition to tap into the realm touched by mediums and mystics. It is interesting that 160 scientists recently took the trouble to denounce astrology. The popular interest in it is tremendous, and shows that there is a great deal more to it than the glib columns in the daily paper.

There are few more interesting or profound books than the *I Ching*. It was not known in English-speaking countries until the late 1800s, and then more as a curiosity to look down on than a source of wisdom. Then in 1949 a superb translation of Richard Wilhelm's German version, which had caught the spirit as well as the letter of the work, was published. Wilhelm had lived the Chinese culture for years, and he had worked with one of the last great scholars of the old school to understand this book which was like the Bible for all Chinese sages since Confucius.

Because of his friendship with Wilhelm, Dr. C. G. Jung was asked to write the introduction. In it he carefully expressed his understanding of the Eastern attitude towards the world as a needed complement to Western causal determinism. He spoke of the difference between nature and the controlled set-up of things in the laboratory, suggesting that there is meaning in variations and "chance coincidence." Jung believed that developing some of the Eastern attitude towards these "meaningful coincidences" is not only healthy, but is the only way to make real use of the *I Ching*.

Three years later Jung completed his important work on the idea of meaningful connections between events that look like coincidences. Later we shall look closer at this principle, which he called "synchronicity." It is basic to

79

understand synchronicity if we are to approach the *I Ching* as a book of great wisdom.

At first the idea did not interest many people. But times have changed, and the *I Ching* has become a perennial bestseller for Princeton University Press. It offers the safest approach to using an oracle because it makes the individual use his own judgment. While oracles do provide insight into a view of the world that is not well known in the West, and also into the capacity and depth of the human mind and psyche, there is danger. People who try to regulate their lives almost totally by oracles avoid developing their own powers of independence and autonomy.

But this danger is certainly not confined to oracles. It is found in most countries of the world where authoritarian policies take over for the individual. Eactly the same danger is found in authoritarian churches, for instance in enthusiastic groups whose members do not think of making a decision without the approval of their director. The fast-growing interest in finding one's own insights, as through the *I Ching,* shows that people today are not satisfied with either scientific, social, or religious determinism, and they are looking for something else.

These types of experiences suggest most of the different ways people have found to experience psi phenomena. They have been known and used by religions all through the ages. On the whole the only safe way to open one's self to these phenomena is with a religious attitude and in a setting that encourages such an attitude in others. An attitude and a setting are needed that will make it difficult for anyone to try to use these experiences to control other people, or for groups to seek an experience merely for the purpose of getting high, perhaps secretly and by using

80

drugs. Even with the safeguard of such an attitude, any but the most natural methods—through religious ritual, visions, dreams, and meditation, should be used with the greatest care. Let us now see what the Judeo-Christian tradition has had to offer about these experiences.

4

ESP in the Bible and Church History

The Bible is a mine of information on ESP or psi phenomena. Nearly every book of the Bible shows the belief that human beings have contact with more than just the physical world and that there are other ways of influencing the world and people besides physical means. Divination and works of power are found throughout the Bible. There is even discussion about what kind of practices are forbidden and why.

Why is this aspect of the Bible so little discussed and understood?

There are first the liberal theologians, who probably have the most to say about what people think in the mainline churches. The most influential of them have maintained that such things as ESP and healing simply did not take place, while other liberals say as little as possible. It is embarrassing to deal with aspects of the Bible that look like non-scientific superstition. One of the main reasons for not taking Jesus' ministry of healing seriously is the fear that looking at it with a critical eye might make Jesus look silly. The feeling seems to be that if we will just overlook these aspects, we can salvage what is good and sensible about the Old and New Testaments.

A slightly more open attitude is found among scholars who believe that extrasensory experiences were recorded in good faith in the Bible, but that they belong to a primitive stage of religion. Once the great prophets came along, it was no longer necessary to have such expressions of more than human knowledge and power. Carried to its logical conclusion, this idea holds that once Jesus of Nazareth, the Son of God, came into the world, man needed no further breakthrough from the divine. Now we live by faith in him alone. This view ignores the book of Acts and the next three hundred years of the church's life. It sees religion as a straight-line evolutionary process. Once a high moral point of view is finally achieved, this takes the place of any need for divine power. These thinkers apparently see no possibility or need for morality and divine power *both* to exist together.

Among various evangelical, charismatic, and conservative groups there is considerable discussion of the occult, of divination, speaking with the deceased, and magic, but most of it is negative. The passages in the Bible condemning these practices are carefully outlined and discussed, but without relating them to the fact that such practices were a part of Old Testament Jewish life, as well as of life in the Greco-Roman world. These passages, arranged in topical order, are as follows: Deut. 18:9-14; 2 Kings 21:5-6; 1 Chron. 10:13-14; Lev. 19:31, 20:6, 27; Isa. 8:19-20; Exod. 7:11-12, 22:18; Mal. 3:5; Acts 8:9-24; Gal. 5:19-21; 2 Tim. 3:8; Lev. 19:26; Isa. 2:6; Jer. 27:9-10; Zech. 10:2; Acts 16:16-18; Rev. 21:8, 22:15; Acts 19:13-16

If these condemnations are taken out of context, the conclusion is that every capacity for psi experience must come from the Evil One unless there is proof that it is a gift directly from God. Sorcery must always be condemned because sorcerers were a part of pagan culture, and they lie and are as evil as adulterers. Turning to the occult is a turning away from Jahweh. Jahweh himself can use these ways of communicating, but the initiative must be entirely on his part. The fact that training may be needed to hear the voice of Jahweh is never mentioned.

None of these points of view looks at the Bible as a whole. These psi experiences are there, and there is no blanket condemnation of any practice as a means of getting to know God's world. The Bible is a practical book. The main point of both testaments is how to get on in a world which is everywhere touched by God's meaning and purpose. How do humans manage in a world which is ultimately dominated by the will of God?

The biblical writers showed little interest in science as the Greeks perceived it, which was to know for the sake of knowing and to let that desire lead one where it may. Thus there is little study of geology, physics, anatomy, psychology, *or* psi phenomena. Our religious forebears were not concerned with understanding either the physical world or parapsychology.

Sometimes a particular practice seemed dangerous, like particular kinds of pagan divination or "augury," and the whole practice was condemned. Sometimes the condemnation was individual. Asa, for instance, died because in his sickness he turned to doctors and not to Yahweh. (2 Chron. 16:12-13). Of course he had to turn to a pagan doctor because there seem to have been none among the Jews. And this, in fact, is the whole tenor of these Old Testament prohibitions and condemnations. They are almost all condemnations of anything that might lead away from dependence on Jahweh.

There is a different flavor in the New Testament. In the Hebrew scriptures the emphasis was more on law

85

than on the New Testament idea of grace. Righteousness could be found by following the law. Retribution was still seen as legitimate for man and God. The New Testament shifts the emphasis to love and forgiveness. The Old Testament Jahweh was seen as a harsh judge who administered both healing and sickness, while according to Jesus, God can be turned to as a loving father *(abba)*, and sickness does not come from him, but is the result of evil forces let loose in the world.[1]

Therefore to the early Christian, healing was good in itself because it was one of the best ways of turning back the works of Evil. In the Old Testament, on the other hand, healings sometimes happened, but they were not a central concern.

There was also a change in the attitude about evil and a new understanding that evil forces, the demonic, are abroad and doing men in. The Old Testament in its concern for monotheism described angels, but avoided saying much about demonic powers. It also said little about a realm with which we could communicate in addition to the physical one. The Old Testament stressed the idea that one must look only to Jahweh. Foreign deities were considered evil and Hebrews were warned not to deal with them. There was therefore, little possibility of a theoretical discussion of psi in the Old Testament, even though the book is full of experiences of it.

The New Testament is not so restrained. It is full of the idea that we are in touch with a spiritual world containing *both* good and evil forces, and that we had better know them and know how to deal with them.

Let us look now at how the experiences were described. I will not be able to cover all of the psi phenomena in the Bible and Christian tradition. I shall try to describe the general attitude of the Bible and the later thought in the church, giving some examples from both.

Divination and Power

There are two kinds of sorcery. One seeks to discover the will of heaven about the present or the future. The other is an effort to influence spiritual and physical powers either to improve a situation or simply to satisfy one's own will. The first action is known as divination, soothsaying, or augury. The second is sorcery or magic, although the same acts may be used for religious purposes. These two kinds of action correspond to the two different kinds of psi we have already discussed, psi which brings knowledge and that which affects results.[2]

The Old Testament reveals a number of different ways to get knowledge of the future or of the will of God. There was first the casting of lots, using the Urim and the Thummim. How they were used is not quite certain, but they are mentioned several times and what was expected was set down quite specifically in 1 Samuel 14:41-42. The teraphim or household gods were also used in some way to ask information from God, but again we do not know the method. Dreams and visions were also seen as ways for God to speak and man to understand the eternal, as I have shown in detail in *God, Dreams, and Revelation*.

In the story of Balaam an omen was used to reveal the presence of an angel, and there are several references to stars as omens of destiny. There is one example of the dead speaking, in the story of Saul's turning to the spirit of Samuel for help. There are also many direct conversations with God and God's messengers (angels) giving information in the Old Testament, as well as the direct contacts with demons in the New Testament. From the call of Abraham to the final vision of the book of Revelation, the Bible is a record of contacts like these with another realm of reality in which information and knowledge were given. In Greek, as we have seen, there were twelve different ways of describing these contacts with something besides the physical world.

There is a basic difference, of course, between magic and religion. Magic is an attempt to use the powers of the spiritual world for one's own ego purposes, while in religious actions like prayer, meditation, and healing, one attempts to be in tune with God's power and to be used as an agent of his loving will. But religion and magic both use the same psi experiences. The religious effort may be to counteract the work of evil forces, perhaps evil magicians, or simply to thread one's way through a seductive world. And this can be accomplished by using an amulet or charm (a symbol), or through exorcism or some other ritual, through cursing or blessing, through symbolic magic, or through the use of plants or animals with special occult virtues.

The *purpose* of the action determines whether it is magic or religion. In religion one is trying to change the fate of the individual by interposing positive factors into his destiny with the help of God. Thus there are times and purposes when religion puts the tools of psi to work, and the relief of sickness is one of them. Sickness is one of mankind's greatest miseries. And since it was seen as caused first by God's disfavor, and then in the New Testament by demonic forces, healing was one of the most important actions of the prophet or seer, the man of God. While the emphasis on healing in the Old Testament is slight, this is one of the central strands in the New Testament, as I have shown in *Healing and Christianity*. How, then, were these contacts and actions, or psi capacities, used in the Old Testament and after that by Jesus of Nazareth?

Gifted Heroes

Although the practice of soothsaying is condemned in certain passages of the Old Testament, the narrative parts show how common and apparently quite accepted these practices were. They were part of the life of the times. How else could God get through except by making himself known in dreams and visions and omens, or in the casting of lots? These were the ways God was heard in the history of Israel. And it was understood that these methods must be available to be used by him. He would be there, and he was jealous of any other use of them.

The history of Israel begins when Abraham listened to a voice speaking within him telling him to leave Ur of the Chaldees and go to a new land. There he was given a vision of the fire passed between the pieces of a sacrifice as the pledge of God's being with him. These patriarchs were sensitive to intrusions from beyond the space-time world and directed their lives by them.

The young Jacob was given the same kind of encouragement when he was fleeing from his brother Esau. In his sleep he saw a ladder ascending to heaven, and from above God gave Jacob the same pledge he had made to Abraham.

The meaning of Joseph's life revolved around his remembering and interpreting dreams. This accounted for his being sold into slavery and then for his release from prison and his rise to power. When he was asked about his ability to interpret dreams, Joseph replied: "Do not interpretations belong to God?" There was nothing wrong with divining by dreams unless one did it falsely or for one's own gain.

Moses, it is recorded, met God face to face. He had no need for difficult and uncertain divination. Jahweh spoke to other men, even prophets, in the dark speech of dreams which they had to struggle to understand. But he surrounded Moses with manifestations of power. Jahweh showed him the bush which burned and was not consumed, and there, with persuasion and magic, he turned Moses into a better wizard than any of the Egyptian sorcerers in order to lead his people out of Egypt. Returning from his experience Moses had another encounter which is not often mentioned in sermons.

> On the journey, when Moses had halted for the night, Yahweh came to meet him and tried to kill him. At once Zipporah [Moses' wife], taking up a flint, cut off her son's foreskin and with it she touched the genitals of Moses. "Truly, you are a bridegroom of blood to me!" she said. And Yahweh let him live (Exod. 4:24-26).

Here is magical practice clear and simple, and directed towards Jahweh himself.

In the book of Judges the same kinds of experiences are described. Gideon put out a fleece, not once but twice, to learn from God that he was going to save Israel. The second time brought a sure sign: the fleece was dry as a bone with dew all around it. Dreams also played a part in Gideon's life.

These great leaders of Israel were seers, which means exactly that in Hebrew. They could *see* farther than ordinary men into a different realm.

For Samuel the voice of God came in the night, but he had to be instructed to listen and respond. Later Samuel did not have to search for Saul to make him king over Israel. Because his father's asses were lost, Saul came to Samuel for help through his clairvoyant ability. Samuel knew what had happened to the asses, and also that this was the young man of whom God had spoken to him.

Priesthood in those days was not very different from the role of seer. The word for priest in Hebrew, *kohen,* is closely related to the Arabic word *kahin* which means soothsayer. People were supposed to go to their priests and prophets who were seers. The prohibition was against going to the pagan temples, where there were also experts who had these abilities. The less sophisticated Hebrews probably had trouble understanding why they had to be different. Outwardly the magic was the same. The story of the adventures of the ark in 1 Samuel shows the aura of magical power which runs through this entire narrative. The seizure of the ark brings evil, and good comes out of its return.

Elijah and Elisha were open to the same kind of power. Elijah was fed by a raven, and he was able to bring down the omen of fire from heaven when the prophets of Baal failed. Elisha saw him carried up to heaven in a chariot of fire and received his cloak. Later Elisha healed Naaman of his leprosy by a ritual washing and gave him some Israelite soil to take home so that he could worship Jahweh properly there. He opened Gehazi's eyes so that he could see the multitude of angels surrounding them. He also made an ax head float in a most unscientific way.

It is popular to think that the great prophets were far removed from such experiences, but the truth is that Amos, Hosea, Isaiah, Jeremiah, and Ezekiel all had visions and were see-ers. Their great insight was to see how morality related to these gifts, and that the gifts of power could be evil if they were not used for God and for moral purposes.

These great men also struggled with the problem of false prophets, false see-ers, and false interpreters of dreams. Many people who had these abilities were in it only for their own profit, or they used these gifts to apply political pressure and curry favor with the leaders. The problem was not with the abilities themselves; it was accepted that God had given them to mankind. The problem was to tell the genuine from the false, and whether people were being led astray by the wrong use. The prophet Habakkuk even gave wise instructions on how to receive and interpret visions. And the book of Daniel goes farther and describes how a prophet and seer became head of the guild of soothsayers in Babylon and still remained such a faithful servant of God that a whole book was written about him.

The power to interpret dreams and deal with the occult was respected and admired, and divining was legitimate if it was done to learn God's will. Most of the heroes and prophet-seers had unusual psi capacities. Having these gifts probably paved the way into the fellowship of prophets. These were men of spiritual power. They were to use it for the good of Israel, for Jahweh, not for their own gain.

In addition, people were not to use these powers without the sanction of the guild of prophets or of the priesthood, and they were forbidden to go to pagans for such help. This is really what the prohibitions in Leviticus and Deuteronomy are about. There can be no question about the existence of these practices in Old Testament times. One does not prohibit what is not going on. But these practices could be dangerous, and people were probably no more level-headed than they are today. And so we find certain prohibitions in the law, which is trying to remove the danger, and bring about a safe order, and keep the Hebrews away from pagan influence.

Jesus as Healer

One reason why so few people in modern times actually look to Jesus of Nazareth for help and guidance is because he is regarded as no more than a great moral teacher, when in fact he was that and something even more. Jesus was a man of power. He was greater than all shamans (a shaman is one in whom the power of God is concentrated and can thus flow out to others). My students begin to see the role Jesus was fulfilling when they read Mircea Eliade's *Shamanism* and Carlos Castaneda's *Journey to Ixtlan.*

Jesus walked on water. He healed the sick and exorcised demons. He knew the future. He calmed the storm, read minds, practiced clairvoyance, and finally arose from the dead. He was in mortal combat with the Evil One. One can hardly understand his ministry, or even something so basic as the Lord's prayer, without an understanding of Jesus in battle against the forces of Evil. In his incisive book, *The Real Satan,* James Kallas has written about the necessity of dealing with the reality of the Evil One if one is to grasp the basic meaning of the New Testament narrative.

Jesus not only used these powers himself, but he passed the same powers of superhuman knowledge, healing, and exorcism on to his followers. As Justin Martyr wrote, "He [Jesus] became what we are in order that we might become what he is." Jesus did not come just to win some kind of spiritual victory in heaven. He came to endow his followers with a new power that would enable them to spread the gospel effectively by using capacities that are out of the ordinary. This is the same kind of psi power Jesus himself had.

At the end of this book I include a list of the passages in the four gospels and Acts showing the various kinds of parapsychological experiences described about Jesus and the apostles.

Paul wrote one of the clearest outlines of the kind of power Jesus gives to his disciples and agents through the Spirit. He explained that these are gifts, *charismata* or powers that are given to enable Christians to live out together the same kind of life Jesus lived with his disciples.

Paul described these gifts, which are capacities beyond the ordinary natural ones, in three different places, in 1 Cor. 12, Rom. 12, and Eph. 4. They range from gifts of healing to those of tongues, interpretation, and prophecy. In addition there are gifts of discernment of spirits, which certainly suggests that people are subject to different kinds of spirits and that it is wise to know enough about them to discern which are from God and which come from somewhere else. The gifts of wisdom and knowledge apparently refer to non-sensory knowledge of heavenly and earthly things. Then there are other gifts like those of leadership, counsel, comfort, and encouragement. These appear to be natural capacities which are enhanced or raised to a new level.[3]

Paul believed that these gifts are given to the apostles and that he himself manifested his share of them. He did not hesitate to tell the church in Rome, "What I am presuming to speak of, of course, is only what Christ himself has done to win the allegiance of the pagans, using what I have said and done by the power of signs and wonders, by the power of the Holy Spirit" (Rom. 15:18-19). It is interesting that Karl Barth, who analyzed this letter point by point in his *Epistles to the Romans,* made no comment on this statement. He could not imagine supernatural power touching anyone but Jesus and continuing on among true disciples.

Yet the risen Christ was so real to the early Christians that they did not always remember which things he had actually said and done during his ministry and which ones he communicated to them after the resurrection in their fellowship with him in prayer. This has created one of the basic problems of New Testament study. The Christian fellowship shared this vivid and nonphysical experience. They were in touch with the spiritual world and with Christ, present and victorious, in it. It appears that almost all Christians who were true disciples were something like shamans in the style of their master, sharing various gifts of power. Many of them exorcised demons and healed. They all knew the Kingdom of Heaven and the reality of the world to come. It is no wonder they spoke so clearly about the communion of saints.

The Acts of the Apostles and Later Christians

The results of contact with the living Christ were set down in the book of Acts. I read it first when I had a period of religious interest as a ten-year-old. It was as exciting as reading *The Wizard of Oz.* When I asked my mother why things like that didn't happen to us, she gave me the answer which I now realize was proper for the daughter of a Presbyterian minister at that time. She answered, "Why, that was a special time. God had to show people that the gospel is real, and he helped a few people heal and see the future, and even raise the dead. But these things were never supposed to go on after we had the church and could learn about these things. What's important now is just to have faith." It was several years before I bothered to read the New Testament again.

The Acts of the Apostles shows that almost every major decision of the apostles—almost every step in the growth of Christianity—was taken because of a dream, a vision, a prophecy, a supernatural visitation, or some kind of divination. The successor to Judas was finally selected by lots along with prayer. Paul was struck down by a vision and then healed and converted by Ananias who was told what to do in a clairvoyant experience. Through the experience of an angel, and later a vision and telepathic information, Peter's ways were changed and Cornelius and a whole group were converted. Paul began his work on European soil because of a dream. Paul had also been present at the stoning of Stephen when the dying apostle cried out that he could see the risen Lord.

The overwhelming experience of Pentecost, with the gift of supernatural languages, was followed almost immediately by the first of a series of healings. The healings included every kind that Jesus had done, from casting out demons and healing physical illness to raising the dead. Paul and Barnabas were even taken to be gods after a cripple was healed in Lycaonia. The people called them Zeus and Hermes and tried to sacrifice to them. Handkerchiefs, aprons, whatever had touched Paul were used to heal the sick. His power through Christ outstripped the abilities of the seven sons of Sceva when they tried to use his methods for their own purposes and had to flee. When he saved a slave girl from demon possession, Paul was taken to court by her masters for robbing them of their oracle and the profit she had brought them.

The prison doors were opened by divine intervention not only for Paul and Silas, whose jailer was converted by the experience, but also for Peter. Several times guilty people were struck down, like the pair who joined the community knowing they had withheld some of their property. The magician Simon was so impressed by the power of the apostles that he offered money to buy the same power, and thus his name was given to the practice of simony, or buying and selling divine favors. When Simon finally realized that the power was a gift from God, he was brought to sincere repentance. A sorcerer who tried to interfere when the proconsul of Cyprus wanted Paul to tell him about Christ was not as lucky.

Over and over the actions of the apostles depended on clairvoyant or precognitive information, prophecies, supernatural visitations, omens and visions, and everywhere they went the same kind of healings and conversions were recorded. Cut out the ESP elements from Acts and the accounts became meaningless. Unless Acts is seen as a book describing the power given by God, such as psi powers and other capacities, the spread of Christianity by a little band of eager but poorly equipped unknowns becomes almost incomprehensible.

Perhaps it is easier to believe that these gifts were not needed by the new church from then on, but this is a naive belief not borne out by the records. In the *Shepherd of Hermas,* for many years considered almost canonical, Christians were told that they were guilty of a sick brother's blood if they knew of the sickness and did not heal it. Everyone of the apologists who stood against the Empire and fought the battle to gain acceptance of Christianity believed in healing and dreams, in supernaturally given information and visions, and in God's power acting through individuals. In one outline of the healings he had seen, written about 170 A.D., Irenaeus listed every one of the kind of happenings found in the book of Acts and the Gospels.

In the next century Athanasius wrote a life of St. Antony, the desert monk, in which his clairvoyance and healing and power over demons were shown to be part of this holy man's life and action. It tells how Antony remarked that, of course, Christians will perform healings, but they shouldn't get puffed up about doing it.

In the fifth century Sulpitius Severus wrote the life of St. Martin of Tours to describe St. Martin's experiences of the same supernatural powers and the healings done by this popular Western saint.

At the same time the leaders of the Eastern church, Basil, Gregory of Nyssa, Chrysostom, and Gregory of Nazianzus, all wrote about the ability of Christians to heal and to gain information about this world and the world beyond by listening to dreams and visions. They noted that the Arian heretics seemed incapable of performing healing miracles like the orthodox.

The Western leaders had the same view and experiences of supernatural abilities. Ambrose, Jerome, Augustine, and Gregory the Great were also men of learning and sophistication who knew these powers themselves. Although Augustine originally believed that healing miracles had ceased, he changed his mind when they began to happen around some relics in his own church in Hippo.

These fathers of the church, who gave Christianity its basic trinitarian foundation, were thoughtful men who knew their intellectual standpoint. The clearest statements of their point of view were given by Gregory of Nyssa in the East and by Augustine in the West.

In his discussion of the Trinity, Augustine pointed out that man has two different kinds of knowing. The individual gets information through sense experience and from memory and it also comes through another faculty which resembles memory but is different. He expressed a theory of psycho-physical dualism with man having capacities of knowing in two different ways, which is the Platonic point of view common to most of the church fathers.[4] Thus they had no problems with psi phenomena. They understood that such abilities are natural to human beings. And like other abilities given to humans, these capacities could be enhanced by God.

The symbol of the Christian Byzantine Empire was given to the Emperor Constantine in a vision, and when the image puzzled him, its interpretation was given in a dream. Eastern Christianity has continued to be open to spiritual reality and psi experiences. The Eastern holy man or *starets* expects such experiences and tries to understand them. *The Way of a Pilgrim,* an anonymous tale of a nineteenth-century Russian pilgrim, gives a good picture of this belief in action.

In the West the lives of saints in every period have been touched by miraculous events and psi happenings. St. John of the Cross was embarrassed by his tendency to levitate, and St. Teresa of Avila and St. Ignatius of Loyola often returned from states of trance with knowledge of another level of reality. Clairvoyant and precognitive experiences, as well as healings, were common among the desert fathers in Egypt, and also among many others. To canonize a saint, in fact, the Catholic Church requires proof of miraculous events attributed to the saint, usually healings, and many of these events have occurred during their lifetime as well as after their death.

In recent years the same kind of experiences have occurred in the charismatic movement which stresses the understanding that God breaks into human life directly and gives these gifts. Beginning among a small group of conservative Bible students, the charismatic experience has spread to most of the major Protestant groups and has now also grown rapidly within the Catholic Church. Wherever it has spread, these groups all speak of the same kind of capacities given to individuals and operating within them. They believe that God speaks directly to people and acts through them in healings, and also in other outer events.

It is interesting to note that researchers who are interested in the connection between psi and religion almost never think of looking for Christian sources of information. The mainline churches have departed so far from the belief that these experiences can happen or should happen that their importance in earlier, vital Christianity is overlooked. For instance Charles Panati and Lawrence LeShan in their books turn to Eastern methods of meditation for material and Robert Ornstein turns to those of the Sufi. The same attitude is found among most young people. It never occurs to them that Christianity has as much of interest and power to offer as other religions. Perhaps it is time for one-sided, intellectual Christianity to take a fresh look at our traditions.

The Christian Framework and Psi Events

As we have seen, all of the experiences which students of ESP are investigating today are found in Jewish and Christian sources and throughout most of Christian history. From Old Testament times on we find examples of clairvoyance, telepathy, and precognition. There are many psychokinetic phenomena, usually healings but also strange meaningful connections between events. People are given experiences of another realm of existence in addition to the earthly one. They are often given comfort by experiences of the risen Christ, or of those on the other side known through the communion of saints. Sometimes experiences of the angelic bring information or offer help when an individual has problems with the demonic. And finally, healing becomes almost the hallmark of a victorious Christianity.

Healing, of course, is the only one of these experiences viewed as a central goal. As in other religions where such experiences are found, the other psi phenomena are all seen as by-products of religious practice and not as goals to be sought. In the Christian framework it is understood that psi experiences are given when an individual turns towards God in need of greater power for consolation or for evangelizing. As we have seen, there is somewhat less agreement about the ways in which these things happen to Christians.

Certain of these experiences are still encountered spontaneously in dreams and visions, particularly by those who consider dreams important and are listening to them and trying to act on them. It must be remembered, however, that some of the most important dreams do not come with power. The experiences of tongue speaking and prophecy can also bring relationship with the area of psi and often bring direction from it. In these cases the experience usually arises from being "in the Spirit" and from group inspiration. Often contact is found through participation in traditional religious rituals like Holy Communion.

In addition, in most ages Christians have followed a practice of meditation which opened them to extrasensory encounters and often to psychokinetic capacities. Much the same practice is still found in Eastern Orthodox monasticism. Western monasticism has largely abandoned such practices, but there are still healing shrines which are visited by great numbers of people.

There is little evidence today or in the past of Christian efforts to seek or induce ESP experiences in the other ways we have discussed. While some mediums have been practicing Christians, the idea either of going to or becoming a medium has generally been avoided because mediumship is thought to be either foolish or wicked. Experiences like those of Edgar Cayce are interesting, but they are just given and cannot be cultivated. The idea of inducing a semi-trance state, perhaps by repetitious ritual or chanting, is sometimes found outside of the mainline of Christian tradition. But Jesus himself put a damper on this idea by telling people to pray in private and not to multiply their requests.

There is no traditional sanction for the use of drugs to alter consciousness and bring contact with the divine as in some religions. Fasting, however, which can have some of the same effects as drugs has been used in many Christian groups.

Christian tradition has no place at all for hypnosis or any method of inducing states of deep trance, although trances of varying depth sometimes occurred at significant times in the Bible. The best known are Peter's trance on the rooftop in Joppa and Paul's experience in the temple in Jerusalem, and Daniel fell into a deep trance before interpreting the king's dream of his madness. States of deep trance also happen occasionally in certain charismatic groups where this is known as "slaying in the spirit." The use of either hypnosis or prayer, however, to give control like this over another person is at cross purposes with the Christian understanding of personality.

For the most part psi events *simply occur* where there is vital Christianity. They are understood to be given because of special need or as a direct result of closeness to the divine and the spiritual. Certain methods of religious observance, including listening to dreams and visions and using them in meditation, may open some individuals to these experiences. The experiences, however, are not valued in themselves but as tools to be used in expressing and furthering the will of God.

If these phenomena are sought for personal gain or power or pride, they become evil. It is not the gifts or experiences of ESP in themselves which are then evil, but the purpose for which they are sought and the way of seeking them. This understanding is important in both the Bible and later tradition. Evil does not seem to be connected with any particular practice or experience, but rather with the method of obtaining it and the way of making use of it. We shall now try to understand these phenomena in relation to the problem of Evil and a view of the world that takes Evil into account.

5

Understanding Psi

Understanding psi, like understanding anything else, means giving it a place in our view of the world. To understand a subject, one must have both scientific knowledge and experience of it, and be able to see how this knowledge and experience fit into what one knows about the world as a whole.

Yet most students of ESP do not see where their experiences fit into the rest of our knowledge. The fact that psi phenomena occur in defiance of all the known laws of physical energy, and even in defiance of time, baffles most people. Most people are as puzzled as Becquerel when he found his photographic plates exposed although he had believed this could not happen. He started Mme. Curie investigating, and then the scientific world had to come up with a new point of view to integrate this knowledge with what was already known. In the end science came up with a whole new picture of the nature of the atom and of matter itself.

It is difficult to know what to do with an experience that does not seem related to other things. Psi experiences act in ways we do not understand. Most objective studies of the subject leave the matter there and confess ignorance. This is an honest and admirable stance. Even Einstein, after 30 years of pondering, could not come up with a mathematical framework to include all the physical data known at the time. He was still convinced that it could be found. "God does not play dice," he said; everything must follow some mathematical order, but he had not yet discovered that mathematical order.

Some students of ESP believe that these experiences will be understood when we know more about physical energy and matter and mathematics. They believe that ESP follows some such law that we have not yet discovered. They do not want to look for any new hypothesis. They do not want to change. After all, it is hard enough to change one basic world view in a lifetime, as T. S. Kuhn suggests in *The Structure of Scientific Revolutions*. It is all right to have faith in an accepted point of view, but it is wise to realize that one is going on *faith* and not on knowledge.

The scientist who maintains that ESP experiences *ought* to be explained in terms of the laws of ordinary classical physics is acting out of faith in rational materialism and failing to deal with all the data that contradict his view. This is one reason why it has taken so long to recognize ESP data as facts. Saying that we will understand them when we have more knowledge of how the world works is no explanation at all. It only says: sit down and have faith in scientific authority. The classical explanation ignores how that authority was changed by the A-bomb and quantum mechanics.

Another group thinks it knows the explanation. These are the religious conservatives who insist that ESP events are all supernatural. They believe that such experiences come from the action of either God or Satan and his hosts and these beings, by definition, we can never understand.

104

According to this point of view these direct intrusions of another world into ours can never be related to our other experiences. Therefore, this group believes that when these experiences come, all we can do is to make the most of those from God and avoid the ones from Satan.

This is another "gap" theory and a kind of scientism based as much on faith as the ideas of the classical scientist in today's world. It *assumes,* with no way of knowing, that the gaps in our knowledge—whatever doesn't fit into the things we do know—can be explained as acts of God and Satan. This explanation really explains nothing. It only sets an arbitrary limit to knowledge, and for anyone with a truly scientific or critical background, it is purely and simply a cop-out. Most scientific advances from Copernicus to Einstein have come only when people have really tried to understand something unknown.

In order to make something like x-ray, electricity, radar, *or* ESP useful one must have some understanding of it. Because lack of understanding surrounds most things with an aura of mystery; they can be turned into tools to control gullible people. To begin to understand, we first need to have a view of the world which will "hold water." Then we can begin to see how ESP might fit in with the other blocks of experience that have gone to build that view, and take the first step towards understanding it.

One hundred years ago scientists felt sure of their view of the world and of man. Popular thinking, which is almost always behind the times, finally caught up with that view and then, like a ship, dropped anchor. And there most people sit, seeing all the knowable universe inside a space-time box which they believe can be understood by our sense experience and by our use of reason. The popular hope is that if we only keep at it long enough, everything will be completely understood in the end. This point of view can be represented by the following diagram:

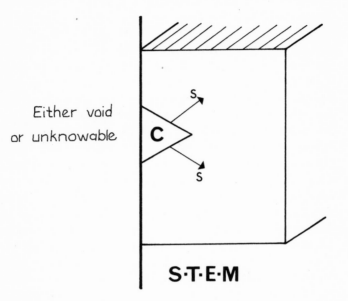

The enclosed box represents the knowable physical world, designated *S-T-E-M* for *space*, *time*, *energy*, and *mass*, the limits of what can be known. The small triangle C represents human consciousness, reaching out into the physical world with the *senses, S,* which bring back impressions known as sensations. Sensations are received and put into rational form by C.

Those who hold this view say either that no elements other than physical ones exist to be experienced, or that there are no others which consciousness can know, depending on the care they use in expressing this idea. This is exactly the view of the universe which ESP and psychokinesis challenge. Apparently there is need for a new hypothesis, or view of how consciousness knows what it can know.

There is other evidence for a new point of view besides psi experiences. I have described this in some detail in *Encounter with God,* suggesting a view which has much in common with the ideas of Plato and Augustine. As they believed, our psyches seem to be bigger and far more complex than we have thought. The psyche reaches into two worlds or realms of experience, instead of being confined to only one. It is like a bridge between two realms. In addition to knowing through sense experience and what is called reason, the psyche has *the unconscious,* which has its own ways of knowing both outer physical events and nonphysical inner ones. What we call ESP is simply one way of knowing the nonphysical realm. In some ways this knowing seems to be more primitive than knowing through regular channels of the nervous system. But as Jung clearly pointed out, in some ways it is far keener and more advanced than our purely physical sense. (This view is diagrammed on p. 108.)

This view gives quite a different picture of how we know and what is available to be known. There is no box around our knowing, only a division. Psi phenomena are those experiences which originate from an area of non-sensory experience. Between this area and the world experienced by our senses is a relationship which seems to be quite different from the relationship of physical causality (cause and effect). It is called synchronicity (the relation of meaningful coincidences) by C. G. Jung and Wolfgang Pauli. This connection or relation seems to suggest that there may be a meaning outside or beyond the system we are considering that gives meaning to both the physical and nonphysical areas of experience.

Jung tells of experiencing such a connection at a crucial time in his development. He dreamed of a man flying towards him who had the wings and coloration of a kingfisher. In order to remember and understand the image,

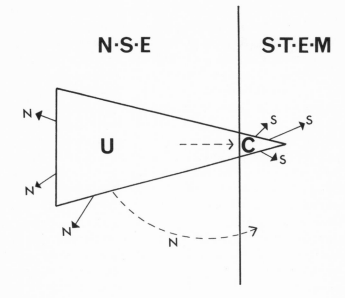

N·S·E   S·T·E·M

Space-Time-Energy-Mass experiences, Consciousness, and the Senses are shown on one side of a central line. On the other side is the unconscious, *(U)*, the part of the psyche which does not get its information through ordinary channels of the nervous system. It extends into a realm of non-sensory experience *(N S E)* which is of the nature of the psyche itself and need not be tied to any concrete physical event. *N* represents ways the unconscious reaches out into both the realm of non-sensory experience and into the world of ordinary sense experience.

he started to paint it, and before the picture was finished, he walked into his garden on the shore of Lake Zürich and found a dead kingfisher. He was astonished, since kingfishers are almost never found near Zürich. In this happening Jung apparently found a clue to the meaning of his dream. Both the *I Ching* and astrology have a similar purpose of revealing clues in one realm of reality that can help us to understand the other realm.

From this point of view the meaning of all experience may come from a center of meaning. But psi experiences themselves are not something from beyond; they are simply natural experiences of the human psyche which mankind shares with other living things and which can sometimes be developed. We are about at the point in understanding them where the seventeenth century chemist was in trying to understand how matter acts and reacts. These experiences are no more irrational than sensations. But to deal with them we need all the analytical and rational skills we can summon up, for they are less understood and therefore more "slippery" than most sense experience. They seem to work on principles different from those of sensory experience.

It is not easy for mature people to grasp this idea of two ways of experiencing and knowing and of two areas or realms that can be known. Children, however, can get it quite easily since they have not been conditioned into believing that the realm of sense experience and physicality is all that exists. I worked for ten years with various students of Jung before I began to understand what Jung was talking about: *human beings are not confined to a physical world*.[1]

The Problem of Evil

In coming to any coherent view of the world one of the biggest problems is the problem of evil and of understanding the nature of evil. Anyone who takes a good look at the outer world and then at the inner psychoid world, finds that all is not perfect in either one. There *are* experiences and events that seem to be meaningful and to lead toward greater consciousness and understanding and care. But there are also catastrophes and experiences that seem to pull the individual down towards disintegration and to lead only to death and annihilation. For people who are concerned with the religious belief that there is basic meaning in the universe, these experiences of destructiveness pose a very serious problem. People reject Christianity and any belief in a creator God because they do not see how a good God could allow all the destructiveness and hatred and chaos that exist in our world.

Several weak excuses for evil have been given by religious people.

Evil is seen as the result of a still-developing universe. According to this idea, once the universe is fully developed, evil will disappear. This is Teilhard de Chardin's view and a flaw in his magnificent vision.

Then there is the belief of Eastern religion that evil is not real, but only illusion, and also the belief of some people that it is just a necessary shadow side of reality, or "the left hand of God" as Alan Watts used to call it. In either case, seeing evil in the world is evidence that a person is still caught in the web of illusion or *maya*. One reason for believing in reincarnation is that it makes sense of the evil which humans experience, because that evil can then be seen as repayment for their moral misdoing in a previous incarnation.

Another explanation with a long history is the gnostic idea that lies behind much Christian thinking. It explains that matter itself is evil, and that man's task is to separate himself from matter by knowledge (*gnosis*) and asceticism. As he does, he will be delivered from being dragged down by evil matter. What this idea as a total view of the universe does to man's view of matter, the body, and sexuality is obvious. It undoubtedly gave rise to the worst of medieval other-worldliness and most of the excesses of Eastern and Western asceticism. Happily, modern Christianity has revolted against asceticism, even though the revolt causes understandable consternation.

110

One more view of evil turns up all over the world in shamanism and was developed to a high point in Persian thought. Judaism came into contact with this idea after the exile, and as I have shown elsewhere, it was a part of the total point of view of Jesus of Nazareth.[2] The basic idea is that there is a creative, loving center of reality, and also a center of destructive and demonic purpose in the universe. These two realities operate in both the physical and the psychoid or spiritual realms of experience. This idea fits the experience of most of mankind. Most of us run up against something that is opposed to the upbuilding, loving, creative concern of God, which seems to cause disasters in the physical world and numinous terror within.

There does not appear to be an ultimate answer as to why God permits this evil, except that—however evil came into being—God as Love cannot use force on it and remain Love. One understanding of how it came to be is that there was war in heaven, as pictured in Revelation 12, and one part of the spiritual world revolted against God and has been causing all sorts of problems ever since.

Although Christianity offers no intellectual solution to the problem of evil, there have been various attempts to solve it intellectually. And these attempts have driven their proponents into one absurdity and heresy after another, mostly because they missed the point that Christianity offers *a way of handling the problem* instead of giving an intellectual solution to it.

In Christianity there is no avoidance of evil or the Evil One. The cross is the central symbol of Christianity, an eternal reminder that the best of men met the worst that Evil can do and came back in the resurrection to defeat the forces of Evil. If the story stopped with the cross, Christianity would be the most tragic faith ever proposed.

Instead, the victory of Jesus is available, and his followers can share in it. They need not be subject to the powers of Evil in either world. This is a practical answer to the problem.

It was also the experience of the early Christians, who found that through Christ they were delivered from Evil which captured and afflicted most people. In the doctrine of the atonement they expressed this experience of being ransomed and delivered.

The experience and doctrine of atonement may be understood from the point of view described in the New Testament and stated by the church fathers. As we have seen, these men found that humans are subject to two realms of experience. In addition, they realized that not only are good and bad found in the physical world, but in the spiritual (or psychoid) realm there are two active forces. These are God and the forces allied to him, and the forces of hatred and death allied to a destructive principle or reality they called the Evil One. The view they expressed is shown in the diagram on p. 113.

From this point of view both of our worlds of experience are influenced by the forces of God and those of Evil. In the outer world we encounter the Evil One in war and plague and unsanitary conditions, in famine, fire, flood, and earthquake. We find the same destructive reality when we turn inward. We find it in hatred, depression, anxiety, neurosis, and psychosis. Few human beings are able to stand up against the negative destructiveness within and not be damaged. They need the protection of the Christ who has demonstrated his power over evil in the resurrection. Let's see how our actual experiences, particularly our psi experiences, fit with this view of the world and this understanding of good and evil.

112

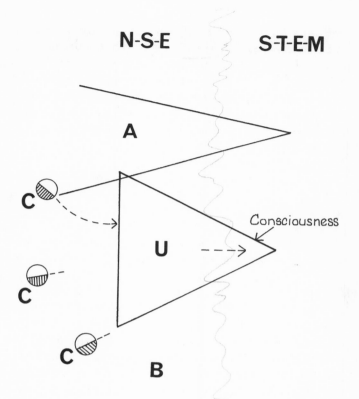

The psyche and the division between two realms of experience are shown as before. *A* stands for the creative and loving center of spiritual reality, which can reach into the physical world as well as touch the psyche directly. *B* represents the destructive principle which affects the psyche directly (like the death wish of Freud), and also moves in the physical world to affect events directly. *C* stands for the centers of spiritual reality which can be attached either to God or to Evil and usually have some of both in them.

Psi and Good and Evil

There is nothing intrinsically evil about the material world, as gnosticism has contended. Nor is there anything intrinsically evil about psi or its use. The experience of

ESP does make us realize that we are not totally encased in a physical world. We can be exposed to the unconscious, that is, to the reality of the spiritual world (on the left in our diagrams). In these experiences one is taken from what seems like the relative security of the physical world and opened to a world where the forces of Evil may be encountered more directly. And it is true that this is dangerous, particularly when the individual who faces these forces within has been lulled into unconsciousness by the Western idea that all spiritual reality is good.

Still, the evil does not lie in ESP, or even in coming into contact with the realities in this other world of experience. The real trouble is our naiveté and an inadequate view of the universe that has tried to convince us that everything is working for good, and that all we must do is to help make it better.

Even Americans are learning that the physical world may not be so secure. In places devastated by war or revolution or ravaged by famine and disease, people might question whether the physical world is secure at all. In both the inner and outer worlds we need to know the dangers and take precautions, just as we try to teach teenagers to drive carefully before we turn them loose on the freeway.

Too often people seem to feel that to be safe from the dangers of the inner world all we need to do is ignore inner realities, but this is far from safe. By ignoring these realities we do not avoid their influence. We simply cut ourselves off from ways of knowing what is going on in the inner world, and this makes it possible for the negative side of inner, psychoid reality to take over.

Hidden, unknown parts of the personality may appear and try to run a person's life. These elements are generally the opposite of what we try to be consciously. Jung has described them as "the shadow" personality which is in all of us. If the shadow elements are recognized and accepted, many of them may be put to work for the benefit of the whole personality and they often become some of the most useful and rewarding parts of one's being. When they are left to operate on their own, however, there is danger of becoming negatively possessed by them so that they work destruction both within and in the outside world.

There are also forces of Evil that seem to be independent of human beings and that seem ready to destroy any time they are allowed a free hand. The risks are too great not to use such experiences as psi wisely and to make an effort to learn all that we can about the realities in the inner world and their power for both good and evil. Using psi experiences naively may be like putting dynamite into the hands of a playful child.

What makes an act, a thought, or an experience good or evil is whether it helps a person participate more fully in the life of God, in love, fellowship, individual growth, and creativity—or whether it draws one more into the orbit of Evil and thus into destructiveness, separation, hatred, and scorn towards one's self or others. Any movement of the soul that opens one to the unconscious, including psi experiences, may make a person more conscious of the forces operating in all of us. And in this way we become less influenced and less easily swayed by the powers of Evil. We can withstand these powers only when we know they are there and can identify them clearly.

ESP experiences may be used either to cheat the process of drawing all parts of the personality into a relation of wholeness, or to further it. If we try to understand the inner meaning of these experiences, they can open us to the reality of the spiritual world and its variety of influences, constructive as well as destructive. And this can help us to become more conscious and more moral. It is practically impossible to know anything about the range of spiritual reality if one acts as if it were not there. Psi experiences certainly make people sit up and take notice of these realities.

Evil is present when any partial good is passed off as the whole or complete good. In the book of Revelation Satan is described as one who thinks he can run heaven better and more efficiently (probably more rationally and with less love) than God. In our social life actions are morally evil when they cause the group to break up and when they harm its members. Thus the whole is not benefited. Psychologically a mood or attitude is evil if it possesses and uses the whole psyche to express its point of view. Organs can function independently of the rest of the body; viruses can use the cells to reproduce themselves; cells can multiply without regard for the need of the organism; and these activities can make the whole body sick. In each of these cases evil takes over when one part takes control of the whole, or pretends to be the whole. This is the essence of evil. When ESP is seen as the central goal and interest of the individual, it too becomes evil. These experiences are useful only in their proper place.

To evaluate our acts and experiences and our lives, we must have some criterion of value. Most criteria are shaped by religious ideas about the nature and reality of God, and there is more variety in these ideas than many people like to believe. Christianity, following Jesus of Nazareth, sees God as essentially love. Actions that lead us to live our own lives in the way and with the kind of love Jesus lived out are morally positive, good actions.

This way of love, however, is not always understood very well. It means trying to know and accept all parts of our being, and the totality of other human beings, as fully as Jesus knew and accepted himself and others. We have to face the shadow side of ourselves as squarely and with

116

as much love as possible and bear the tension of trying to integrate these often dark and opposite elements into a whole, well-rounded personality that is able to know and to give acceptance and love.

In the East, on the other hand, impersonal consciousness or the Divine Mind is seen as the goal. The most perfect and moral actions are those that help one to pull away from emotion and to merge into the impersonal sea of Cosmic Mind.

In *Myths to Live By* Joseph Campbell gives an excellent picture of the difference between these two views of the universe. Merging into union with Cosmic Mind is a far different goal from relating to unbounded love. Christianity requires a different mode of living. The accent is not only on what I can *become,* but on what I can *do* and *be* to facilitate life and development in those around me. Instead of a circular orbit around a single point, there is an elliptical one around two different points.

Evaluating Psi Experiences

From a Christian point of view psi experiences are valuable or valueless depending on whether they help one to meet and know and express the love expressed in the life and death and resurrection of Jesus. Do these psi experiences help me in seeking freedom from possessive Evil for all people, including myself? When an experience supports this goal it has value. But if ESP experiences hinder this goal, they are dangerous. There are several pitfalls into which those with psi abilities may fall:

1. *Using psi for personal power or profit.* This is dangerous whether one is trying to gain prestige, popularity, power over others, or money. To be safe psi must be used humbly. People who advertise or exploit this kind of gift

are asking for trouble. And since psi is a powerful and often admired gift, the danger is proportionately greater. Using psi in this way may result in a disastrous ego trip.

2. *Using psi to harm the user or another.* Obviously, using psi to express hatred or destructiveness would make it the very essence of evil. Black magic is the conscious use of psi for ends of destruction. Few of us would consciously use psi in this way, but all of us have hidden and not-so-nice motives that may be turned loose and do damage to ourselves and to others. We may think that our use of psi is harmless, but if we are motivated by unconscious destructive feelings our use of psi may serve destructive purposes.

The first task is to know one's feelings and motives as clearly as possible so that they can be kept in sight and dealt with creatively. There is danger in unconsciousness. We may even be unconscious that we are reaching out in telepathy or communicating other psi effects and still touch other destructively through such experiences.

3. *Letting fraud or deceit creep into the use of psi.* One must admit that these abilities come and go, and that the only way one can be sure of psi information is to let it be tested by the facts of experience. No one can be sure of a precognition, for instance, until the event has happened. Many predictions miss the mark, and there is danger in allowing wishful thinking to fill in the gaps in one's performance. The task again is to use the gifts humbly, honestly, and *consciously.* Whenever we try to make ESP more than it actually is, we lead ourselves and others astray. Dishonesty is never creative, and dishonesty may be conscious or unconscious.

4. *Encouraging psi abilities by less natural methods.* Experiences of ESP that come through dreams, religious rit-

uals, and meditation appear to have far less dangers than those forced by the use of drugs, trances, and hypnosis. If one has become open to psi by these methods, it is wise to have the guidance of established religious rituals in using the abilities.

5. *Thinking that one is strong enough to control any force encountered in the spiritual world.* This is a form of pride that leads to disaster in both the inner and outer worlds. Becoming inflated about any kind of personal power usually brings trouble, and pride about psi is no different from pride about other things. It goes before a fall.

6. *Using psi just for the experience itself,* apart from a religious attitude towards life. These experiences are not the same as ordinary experiences. The tendency to get caught in fascination with them makes it doubly important to know one's religious stance. In addition, one can seldom create from scratch the kind of religious attitude that is needed. Our best safeguard is to test these experiences against the basic ideas of the New Testament and to ask if one's use of the practice is in agreement with the New Testament.

7. *Using ESP to lord it over other people,* to dominate them consciously or unconsciously. Any religious capacity becomes destructive if it is used to keep people in subjection to authority. Because of the strange and unusual nature of this gift, it presents unusual temptation to use it for control of other people. Those who have this capacity need to be very careful that they do not exploit those who do not have it and who are awed by it.

8. *Using ESP to judge people who do not have these abilities.* If one looks down on people who have not experienced psi, it is very easy, consciously or unconsciously,

to consider them second-class citizens. Psi ability is then substituted for love as the real goal. The essence of evil is putting secondary values ahead of primary ones. This problem is not limited to psi, of course. Tongue speakers, and also gifted people in other areas, sometimes think that those who do not have the same gifts are not as spiritually advanced. Our expression of psi ability, like any other, needs to be constantly measured against the central criterion of love.

How can we know, then, when it is helpful, creative, and permissible to use ESP capacities? The best test is probably to ask one's self these questions:

- Does my expression of this ability spring out of love?

- Does it come from the kind of love that wants me to know the world and human beings as they are, and tries to help me accept myself, the world, and other people in this way?

- Does it result in an increase of this love, promoting psychological, intellectual, and spiritual growth, both in myself and others?

- Can I see healing effects on individuals—body, mind, and soul—and in strengthening and building up the group of which I am a part?

- Is there an increase of hope and faith and joy, and do I see others given courage and liberated to discover their own gifts and talents?

Using psi is certainly good and valuable when one can answer *yes*. These results seem to occur most often when ESP phenomena happen within a church setting and are given a definite place there. They can then bring individuals who have these capacities into touch with another realm of existence so that they meet face to face the Love that is found there. By bringing back a taste of love and hope and faith, they can help to empower the whole group to become instruments of that Love. This is up to the people of our churches, however, and each of us can help by keeping an eye on our own specific situation.

The same criteria may be used in judging the use of any gift or ability. The ability to make money may be more dangerous than ESP when it is separated from religious standards of value. I am certain that political charisma is far more dangerous. Intellect turned loose from other values can be demonic, as C. S. Lewis shows in *That Hideous Strength,* his horror thriller set on a college campus. Beautiful singing voices, with no control on ego inflation, have sometimes split churches open and turned people away from God.

The idea that ESP is in some way a particular avenue for Evil is not true. We need to be aware of evil and unconscious power in all ordinary things, rather than avoiding Evil by looking for it only in special places and special talents. Evil is far more complex and insidious than this. Evil is not inherent in money or ESP or power, but in putting something other than Love at the center of life.

The idea that things like the occult are sources of Evil hides the real nature of God, as well as of Evil. People are diverted from the main task of knowing Christ's love and expressing it. They are often led to condemn the wrong thing and thus become agents of Evil themselves. This makes it very dangerous to see evil concentrated in any one thing.

ESP may be dynamite, it is true, because it does open one to the spiritual world. But money and power are just as dangerous. And egoism that values everything in terms of self-interest is more centrally evil than all three.

People who come to know themselves well enough so that they know how to reach out to other human beings soon realize that few human actions spring from pure motives. Our motives are nearly always mixed; this is one reason why we need humility. One may not realize that ESP or money or power or intellect, or even meditation, is being used for motives potentially evil. But deep within each of us are roots of selfishness and lack of concern for others that are difficult, if not impossible to eradicate.

In each of us there is personal evil for which we are individually responsible. It is up to us to do the best we can to know and to avoid it. As parts of society and the human race, most of us also find that we share in the collective evil of our society. For example, people brought up in a society using slavery may not realize that they participate in the evil of slavery just by being a member of that society. In a world that uses war to settle conflicts no one is totally blameless. Because of this deep stain in each of us, no gift or ability is ever perfectly pure. If it is something as powerful as ESP, one must use real care.

First of all one can try to eliminate any personal motive that would destroy the value of this gift like using it for financial profit or to control other people by trying to get guidance for them.

But then one needs to look deeper into the psyche and realize the collective pressures and evils that so often take over when we are unconscious of them. No one can oppose these evils singlehandedly, but at this point the Risen Christ is ready to help us if we will turn to him. Acting compulsively or with cruelty, and then saying "The Devil made me do it" is the ultimate cop-out and self-deception. Our task is to go as far as we can in knowing and cleaning up our own motives, and then to ask for the help Christ is able to give to free us from the evil that operates in and through us. Evil may be suggested to us by the demonic, but if we act on the suggestion and do something which injures others, we have no one to blame but ourselves. We may need to look deep within and become more conscious

122

of the roots of evil. At the crucial point it is our responsibility to call for help so that evil will not use us.

Extrasensory perception, then, opens up a whole new view of spiritual reality and the soul. If it is isolated from our religion and our central values and used for doubtful motives, it becomes demonic and an instrument of Evil like any other valuable human capacity. But psi ability may also become a powerful aid in eliminating the evil that is so much a part of our lives. It may be used to know God and to serve him. These experiences may well be necessary to help us understand the forces that play on us and reach a state of consciousness where we can become truly responsible.

6

ESP, Theology, and Christian Living

What is the significance of clairvoyance, telepathy, precognition, healing, and psychokinesis for Christian thinking and Christian living? If these experiences are real and if they are natural phenomena, this question must be answered because it has many implications for what a Christian thinks and does. How, then, are Christians to deal with ESP?

The first and most obvious task of the intelligent Christian is to be informed about this significant area of research which has so many implications for the reach of the mind and for one's capacities for religious knowing. People today show a legitimate longing for spiritual experiences. Their interest in Eastern ways of meditation, in mystical experience wherever it can be found, their use of drugs, and practices like the *I Ching* all speak of their desire for experience outside of the space-time box.

This is something they have a right to expect from the church. But the church cannot touch this longing until it is equipped to open up ways of finding such experiences. We send missionaries equipped with more than just good will to parts of Africa that need to grow more food. To

124

love the African means to meet his legitimate need. To love sophisticated Westerners means trying to understand where they are and to meet their need. People today are starved because they are not satisfied by bread alone. They need more than physical satisfaction. They need spiritual satisfaction as well.

A world view that deals only with a physical world and the five senses does not satisfy inquisitive and perceptive people today. They have begun to explore and they know that there are all sorts of signs that point beyond such a view.

Ignoring such signs as the data on ESP puts Christians almost back to the Middle Ages when the theories of Copernicus could be denied and study of the human body was almost thwarted to keep the belief system intact. But in the end those beliefs became equated with superstitious wish-fulfillment and many of the best minds ignored the church and its wisdom. Modern men and women show a similar tendency to go right ahead seeking experiences on their own and treating the church's message as irrelevant.

Christianity grew up with a world view that included the kind of experience people are looking for, and this view offers an understanding of such experience that is lacking in the modern world. Unquestionably it will take some work to make that understanding available to people today, and some Christians may have to review and change their way of looking at the world.

This change may be painful, but the study is fascinating and can open up refreshing new insights. Popular books on science and parapsychology continue to appear, and there are several readable books on the important ideas of C. G. Jung. These all help in getting a picture of the world as people today, particularly the younger generation, are coming to see it. Christian thinking can then be

125

communicated in a way that will be heard and can help to direct experiences and people's attitudes towards them.

Religion and psi must be handled with critical rational evaluation. Neither the data nor the conclusions of those who have developed the data need be taken at face value without scrutiny. They need to be questioned, analyzed, and the facts integrated. This is no time for suspension of our rational faculties. We need to use those faculties to deal with the new kind of data, and then try to develop a world view that includes the new data with the old. The function of reason is not to deny or produce facts, but to see which experiences have actually been tested and verified, and then try to relate them to the rest of one's experience.

As we have seen, researchers have a tendency to look for Eastern models of thought about these experiences because current Christianity has so little to say about them. This can certainly be changed by Christians who are not afraid of psi experiences and know the history of their own tradition.

Real knowledge about psi and its implications can change the atmosphere of fear about these experiences. Once people realize that there is good reason to believe in the reality of the New Testament experiences, we may even find it easier to change our familiar ways of theologizing and philosophizing. If medieval Christians had been more sure of their experience of the transforming power of the risen Christ, they would not have been so terrified of the discoveries and the theories of Copernicus. If we can accept the data of parapsychology, we will try to understand the effort of physical science to make sense of these experiences. Then we will not be afraid, even though the facts cast real doubt on some of the ideas of Western theology since the growth of scholasticism, and on much of Western philosophy since the time of Descartes.

The Platonic view of the world, with which Christianity grew up and became triumphant, is still available. If we are willing to integrate such a view with the one that parapsychological facts suggest, Christianity will again be in a position of central influence on modern culture. L. L. Whyte made the same suggestion in his brilliant book *The Unconscious Before Freud.*

We have seen that there are various ways of opening oneself to parapsychological experiences, and that some of them present real dangers. Atomic physics also carries with it incredible dangers. Yet we do not let fear of the atom bomb stop us from trying to learn about the atom and find other ways of releasing its power. We can become more creative, as well as more dangerous, the more our knowledge increases. ESP shows us possibilities of new reaches of human knowing and power within man. These phenomena need to be experienced within a religious group where men and women respect them but are not afraid to explore them. The two safest approaches are through dreams and spontaneous visions that open this area up naturally, and through meditation and religious ritual.

Medical men, as we have seen, even find dangers in meditation. This attempt to withdraw from total preoccupation with the world of sense experience, if practiced too long at a time, may lead to disorientation. It may also lead into experiences of another realm where one is helpless to act and may even be overwhelmed. No inner journey should be undertaken without guidelines from those who have been that way before and returned in a better state than they were before they undertook the journey. The wisdom of the church offers valuable guidance.

Individuals may feel the need to try other methods

which can be approached safely only if these are attempts to seek reality and are regarded with scientific objectivity. The one thing that will not work is for a person to play around in the area of psi experiences. There is great need for religious wisdom and understanding, for the values and the fellowship the church offers, as well as for objectivity. Scientific exploration of psi also needs the guidance of religious values. The tragedy of Hiroshima, for instance, shows the need for communication between science and religion. But Christianity can have nothing to say about psi exploration unless it knows what is going on and what it means!

Psi Theology

The implications of psi phenomena for theology are many. They suggest a new view of experiences of God and so of the value of meditation. They reaffirm the validity of the New Testament narrative. Christian healing again becomes sensible. Factual reasons can be shown for believing in immortality, and for taking Christian morality seriously. Altogether a new thrust is given to the idea of ministry and to the training of those who are to minister. Let us look briefly at each of these implications.

The moment we realize that psi knowledge is a fact, we become free from the idea that our knowledge is all confined to a space-time box. If ESP can bring knowledge of physical events that can be verified, we need not deny people's statements about experiences of a nonphysical world. These experiences, described in every culture, must then be considered. It is up to serious students of religion and the religious life to study them and to see if any consistent pattern emerges from the descriptions. Statements about religious experiences become necessary data for understanding our religion. It becomes almost absurd to decide what religion is, or ought to be, only by working with concepts and ideas about it on the basis of rational reflection.

People have all kinds of experiences, and there is only one way to find out what their statements may express about the nature of reality. This is to sift through the experiences and see what conclusions they suggest about spiritual, and also physical, reality. The task of trying to make sense of this infinitely complex data of experience is not an easy one. This has been the task of all the great historical religions. Christianity has also tried to provide a view of reality in this way, particularly during the first four or five centuries of its life. Dr. Jung has again tried to perform the same task, as David Burrell shows in his *Exercises in Religious Understanding*.

This is a two-part task, which must include comparison with the conclusions of the past. Trying to start from scratch to develop an adequate religious framework from our own experiences would be like looking at the stars and the activity of atoms and trying to come up with a theory of relativity and quantum mechanics without knowing geometry and mathematics and physics. Human beings need their cultural heritage to deal with their experiences either of science or religion. When they ignore this heritage of experience, they are very likely to produce nonsense.

As we begin to take inner experiences seriously and learn about the reality of the psychic world, we find facts about the world and ourselves that give a different picture of the universe from the familiar one most people believe is true. We are familiar with the idea of a closed and orderly universe that ticks along like a self-winding watch. This is the kind of universe Einstein was thinking of when he insisted that God does not play dice, and he tried for years to come up with a theory that would demonstrate this kind of mathematical order in all things. He saw no

129

place for a center of meaning that could relate to each individual in an individual way. He did not believe that the principle of our universe could be the same kind of purposeful life force found in some individuals, often in experiences of ESP and particularly psychokinesis.

These experiences, however, help us to realize that the psychic world is a real world which is not totally tied to the physical one, and that we live in an open universe. They show that human personality has direct and observable, although finite, effects on the physical world. Once this is accepted, it is easier to realize that there is a psychic or spiritual reality beyond the human which also has such effects. We then have good reason to believe that we can be in touch with a reality like ourselves, but infinitely greater than the human being, from which the image of the human being was struck. This reality appears to be the organizing principle of the world. Not only can this principle deal with logic and mathematical law, but it deals personally with human beings as well.

Indeed the experience of those who have known most deeply the realities of the Christian gospel, speak of meeting this principle as the risen Christ. They describe encountering a love which will go to any length to reach and touch and transform human life. These individuals have also described how they were then filled with a new understanding of their destiny and purpose, and were given new power to put that kind of love into action.

There are also experiences of an aspect of reality which frustrates and draws the individual away from this goal. It lures him into separation rather than fellowship, into death rather than life, into hatred rather than love, into destruction rather than creativity.

No religion other than Christianity deals seriously with this experience of down drag, and no other has offered a solution to its negative effect and its power. This evil is

130

not an illusion of man and is not dependent upon either the physical world or on occult phenomena, but is clearly a principle that constantly tries to put some secondary value in place of the reality of love as expressed in Jesus of Nazareth and by him. Over the ages his followers have described meeting this principle of evil and how they have been given the power to resist it by the risen Christ.

These encounters with Love and also with Evil were described from apostolic times through the centuries of persecution, and also by the teachers of the church who expressed them in theological form. Most of the men and women we call saints have spoken of the same experience of God. It is expressed in classical form in the poetry of St. John of the Cross and Francis Thompson, as well as in 1 John 4 and Paul's ode to Love in 1 Corinthians 13. Von Hügel describes it in his remarkable study of the life of St. Catherine of Genoa, *The Mystical Element of Religion.* And this encounter is still available to men and women who seek it. As I have tried to show in my book on meditation, *The Other Side of Silence,* most of us can use this practice to become open and know the reality of the Loving Christ. ESP reminds us that such experience is real and that it may be one's most important experience.

ESP and the New Testament

These encounters after the resurrection were crucial in the New Testament. Knowing that Jesus could communicate with them made it possible for a defeated and frightened group to hold together and wait for something to happen. Then, as they found, there are other experiences which come to those who are open and trying to live in accordance with that Love which the disciples knew. Dreams and revelations often come that show something specific when specifics are needed. One finds a new power

131

to discriminate between the creative influences of love and those of evil, a power which Paul called the discernment of spirits. Capacities are given to bring healing to the body and to the mind, and also to bring consolation. These capacities also help us to use our intellects more creatively, and to deal with administration more effectively. Individuals are given the gift of speaking in tongues, which has many meanings but at the very least is a kind of praise that goes beyond the bounds of any words or rationality.

New Testament critics have tended to play down this element of creativity and power, or even to go along with Bultmann and question whether such things ever happened. The new study of psi phenomena changes the picture. If people will look at the facts about human powers of communication and action, they need not be upset by doubts that were so obviously caused by ignorance. Like everyone else at the beginning of this century, biblical students had only the limited facts of nineteenth-century science to guide them. They could not conceive of experiences like those described in the New Testament. Today we are more fortunate in having a science that has learned more about the universe and how many things are possible in it.

If human beings, under ordinary circumstances, have powers like the ESP abilities experimenters have described, is there any reason to deny that similar things could have taken place in New Testament times? Those who believe that the Spirit of God touches and empowers individuals, and even groups of people, will realize that the gifts and abilities described in the New Testament are quite possible.

At the same time there is no reason to lay aside our reason and analytical faculties and accept everything as fact without looking at what is described objectively. Wholesale acceptance is almost as foolish as blanket rejection, particularly when so much material is becoming available for comparison. For instance, Franc Newcomb's description in *Hosteen Klah* of how the Navajo shaman turned a tornado aside gives a modern-day example much like Jesus' calming of the storm. Eliade's *Shamanism* shows how many parallels to the New Testament experiences are found in other religions. The laboratory data on clairvoyance and precognition can be compared with the stories about Jesus—how he knew the disciples would catch a fish with a coin in its mouth, how he sent them ahead to find a donkey in a certain place, and later told them exactly the things that would lead them to an upper room suitable for them to meet for the Passover, as well as his predictions of his death.[1]

Stephen's vision of God as he was stoned can be taken quite seriously, and God can speak to us today as he did to Paul in visions of the night. Paul listened when he dreamed of a man of Macedonia pleading for help, and this started his work in Greece. And when an angel told him what would happen during a storm aboard ship, he reassured the crew. Peter's healing of a cripple at the Beautiful Gate does not look nearly so improbable when we realize that nurses are successfully using therapeutic touch and a psychiatrist speaks of faith having as much power as penicillin in some situations. The experiences of tongues and of prophecy can also be seen as genuine expressions of another realm of experience. Most of our doubts about the experiences in the New Testament have arisen simply because the old-fashioned science kept us from seeing the world as it actually is. When psi is understood, it can remove the blinders from our eyes.

What is more, our view of these experiences is no longer limited to the New Testament and the lives of the saints. They can become a part of modern Christian practice. There is a place for the ministry of Christian healing and for training in that field, and also in traditional Christian ways of approaching the psyche through meditation and listening to dreams. There is a place for schools that teach about the psyche. Our Christian tradition is rich in ways of helping people become open to the positive aspects of the nonphysical world. People hunger for this understanding, and in many places they look to the church in vain for instruction.

There is also need to train people in the discerning of spirits and in ways of helping those who suffer with neurosis. Neurosis may well be as much a spiritual disease as a psychological one. This has been pointed out, not by a theologian, but by C. G. Jung, a psychiatrist who was the disillusioned son of a minister. These people need to learn how to work with dreams and visions and interpret the images that arise in both.

In short, many of the experiences described in the New Testament can become vital agents for restoring and transforming people's lives today. As such experiences are shared with an effort to understand them, we will discover many things that point to the reach of our psyches beyond either space or time. It takes only a few of these experiences (for instance, a vision of a dying friend, or hearing a person ask for help at the moment of suffering an accident in a distant place) for people to realize that there is a strong possibility that the psyche lives on after death. The reality of the Christian faith then becomes very apparent. And I have found that there is no better clincher for understanding our need for Christian morality.

Again, this does not mean believing any experience that is reported, either present-day or in the New Testament, without using our best abilities to study and evaluate them. But the range of experiences likely to be found makes the claim of charismatic Christians far more reasonable.

ESP and the Ministry

Once we realize that people need religious experience and not just intellectual doctrine, a new kind of training for ministry is indicated, one with the accent on helping people further their growth and development. I am not suggesting, however, that those who minister can get along without using their rational minds. They need the best training they can get in logical reasoning and the critical evaluation of data.

And since rational theology is important, those preparing to deal with people in the modern world should know enough about significant developments in that world to be sure their theology makes sense in terms of our present knowledge. They should have at least a passing acquaintance with the philosophical implications of atomic physics and quantum mechanics. They also need some real knowledge of psychosomatic medicine, depth psychology and parapsychology, including books like Jerome Frank's *Persuasion and Healing,* Jung's *Memories, Dreams, Reflections,* and Panati's *Supersenses,* as well as Heisenberg's *Physics and Philosophy* and Eliade's *Shamanism.* Where actual facts raise doubts about theology, much of that rational theology may need to be rethought and supplemented.

This is not all that is needed, however. In his survey of people who had mystical experiences, Andrew Greeley reported that the minister or priest was the last person with whom they would share a mystical experience. Clergy are not being trained in the very thing they need to know. Our Christian traditions offer the wisdom, and also methods, for dealing with the realm from which such experiences come. Yet people who encounter this realm within themselves usually find no one to turn to except a psychiatrist, and few of them are trained to understand and work

135

with Christian traditions. There is need for clergy who have learned to deal with the larger psyche revealed by ESP, and also with those experiences of another realm of reality which this larger psyche reveals.

It is not easy to lay aside the idea that ministry means dealing simply with consciousness, rationality, and problems laid out in the open in this world. In many places clergy are still being prepared on this basis. Often they are taught only to give an intellectual grasp of the Christian faith and to offer some crisis counseling. If the human mind and personality were nothing more than rationality, conscious intention, and will, this nineteenth-century model would be enough. As psi experiences show, however, human beings are far more complex, and if pastors are to learn to work with the totality of the psyche, a different approach must be provided.

Christian history and recent science offer suggestions for the kind of training that is needed. The early church required three years of instruction and experience before baptism. This training was based on an understanding of human personality, expressed by the fathers of the early church, which is quite similar to the approach provided by the depth psychology of C. G. Jung and his followers. This is not surprising since Dr. Jung often worked with early Christian ideas. His approach to the psyche takes psi potential into account. It gives guidelines for understanding the nature and structure of the psyche and how its growth and development can be encouraged. When this scientific approach is joined with the insights of the early church and the masters of the devotional life, an understanding of personality emerges that suggests ways of preparing individuals to guide and minister to others in today's world.

Psi data reveals essentially the same picture of the human psyche, and also the kind of world with which we all interact and the rich variety of experience there is for us to deal with. When those who minister to others realize the implications of that experience, people who have had mystical encounters will turn to the church rather than hiding them or looking to Eastern religion. The traditional wisdom of the church, collected over two thousand years, will help open up the meaning of these experiences. Since few individuals discover much of this wisdom on their own, modern religious leaders need to know this material and how it relates to various individual experiences. They also need to know the ways of spiritual direction in the past, the methods that have been used and what can be learned from the various saints in the past.

The understanding of human beings which was used intuitively by spiritual directors in the past has been given form by recent discoveries in the field of human dynamics. This approach can now be learned in a more systematic way through an intern-type program. In such a program the individual learns to work in various areas, particularly in the area of dreams and imaginative meditation. These are both ways of helping people to know the depth and complexity of their personalities and what is met in many layers within the human psyche. Some of the more unconscious layers affect people's outer behavior, sometimes give them extrasensory perception, and often open them to an experimental relation with God. It is impossible to direct a person's spiritual life without knowing these levels, first of all within one's self. Our rational, cognitive minds are important, but there is more to us than that. This is particularly true in religion.

A doctor learns to detect heart trouble only by listening to hundreds of hearts. The way to learn about the depth and complexity of the human psyche (its amazing range of moods, emotions, perceptions, and abilities) is to be trained in listening to other people and also in listening to one's self. One can lead another person only as far as one has been led himself. The blind cannot lead the blind. An analyst can help others only after being analyzed, and the spiritual director only by having been directed. The process of training shamans is quite similar and requires several years of apprentice training, as Carlos Castaneda describes in *Tales of Power.*

Human beings, however, will not reveal the depth of themselves to another until a relationship of trust is developed. Only in the presence of caring will a person let another into the innermost sanctuary of his heart, into his pain and anxiety, ecstasy and joy. This citadel cannot and should not be forced. Religion flourishes only in the presence of self-giving, *non-judging* love. Besides one-to-one encounters, experiences of interpersonal relationship in a group setting can be helpful. In this way individuals who are coming to know their own depth and potential begin to share with others and thus become equipped to lead others to their own inner depths of meaning.

Those who seek to guide others on this way need to be equipped intellectually with a world view that is more adequate than the nineteenth-century one of rational materialism. The nineteenth-century thinkers did not try to deal with doubt. Instead the thinkers of that time did all they could to conceal doubt under the cloak of a positivistic attitude, and there it was left to grow and spread until doubt has become a disease in our society, infiltrating both the church and theology.

To help people find experiences of the divine and lead them into active ministries of consolation and healing, one must be familiar with the developments of Western thought that suggest that a meaningful relationship to God is possible in our time, and that this idea is not born out of a return to the womb of wishful thinking. One must start from an understanding of Enlightenment and post-Enlightenment thought and come to a base that will give people reason to listen to their desire for deeper experience.

It is helpful to know something about those who have had the deepest experiences in the past. When individuals learn that these experiences were almost the norm in another age, they find it much easier to accept and work with the same things in themselves.

There is probably no better way of going at it and learning about the depth and power of our psyches than by trying to understand our dreams. They reveal many of our half-conscious attitudes which we prefer to avoid, as well as other attitudes of which we are almost totally unconscious. In fact, dreams can give a picture of the whole psyche, including our ways of relating to God. One of the fields of study for those preparing for this kind of ministry and service is that of learning to use dreams to understand what is in the deeper levels of the psyche, both in one's self and in others.

An understanding of psi phenomena makes necessary a new idea of the origin and development of human beings, and also of the universe itself. The most adequate model is not very different from that of Jesus and the early church. This understanding of ourselves and our world suggests the religious training we have been considering and the need to develop understanding in the four areas we have discussed. The Christian ministry I am suggesting requires, first, an understanding of the depths within one's self and in others; second, learning how to develop and deepen one's direct relationships with others; third, developing understanding that there is a religious reality to which one can relate and learning a way to relate to it; and finally, coming to a world view that admits such a reality and a way of knowing it, and that can be presented to a skeptical and positivistic world.

The basic goal is to provide the church with men and women who can know the Love of God available to them in Christ and who can learn to express it to those around them, and are also able to support their practice and their view of the way God is known without being defensive.

Concluding Observations

Human beings are far more sensitive to one another than most psychology suggests. Once we realize this fact, it is easier to see how much our attitudes can affect other people even when they are not expressed out loud. Feelings of hostility and disdain, of judgment and condemnation, no matter how well hidden, can be experienced by others. *Homo sapiens* is no less sensitive than rabbits and mice and shrimp and plants. It is important for me not only to realize my destructiveness and contain it, but to come to terms with it inside myself. I have far more influence on others than I sometimes think.

One of the basic results of the study of children by depth psychologists is the realization that children often live out the unfaced attitudes and desires of their parents. People lay a heavy burden on their children when the path of unconsciousness is chosen. When the problems it causes show up before the child is grown, getting at them is mostly a matter of treating the parents. As Frances Wickes details clearly in *The Inner World of Childhood,* the parents' unconscious attitudes often have far more influence on children than their conscious expressions.

What is true of parents and children is potentially true of all other human relationships, although usually to a lesser degree. Christian morality clearly requires each of us to deal with our own inner chaos so that it will not slip out of its space-time container and affect others in extrasensory ways. Sometimes I find it helpful to paraphrase

140

the Lord's Prayer and ask, "Forgive us our unconsciousness as we forgive the unconsciousness of others."

In addition, if a person has the capacity to heal others through sacramental or caring action, there is an equal moral responsibility. If one fails to take the healing action, one is an offender, perhaps even, as the *Shepherd of Hermas* suggested, guilty of the sick brother's blood. We have almost incredible capacities to heal and to help others become open to fulfill themselves. We need to use these abilities or we are delinquent for omission, as much as for what we do amiss.

Life after death is a subject the church has avoided as much as possible ever since Copernicus overthrew the medieval view of hell and heaven, and these places of the after-life could no longer be located in physical space, within and above the earth. Now, however, our awareness of psi phenomena is helping to change our world view once more, and we have begun to realize that reality does not always conform to our ideas of space and time. Once the psyche is understood as one of the elements in this world that can transcend space and time, death begins to lose its tyranny. Since the psyche is apparently more than is expressed by its physical envelope, the destruction of that physical container does not necessarily end everything. Both psi experiences and the experiences of the church fathers suggest that our psyches go on existing after death, and this requires a new understanding of death and how our lives can be lived with some thought for what may happen afterwards.

The subject of death is no longer taboo in Western society, but it cannot be dealt with adequately until we have an understanding of life after death. Psi experiences make us look at ourselves and at death differently. They make us realize that our psyches have access to a realm of experience independent of ordinary cause and effect, and

141

that this part of our being may not be subject to the kind of generation and decay observable in the physical world. There seem to be good reasons for believing that the psyche goes on after death, and this provides us with a profound view of life itself.

If the church does not take ESP data seriously and integrate these experiences into its thought and practice, people will deal with them without the wisdom and understanding that the church can provide. When Mary Baker Eddy tried to tell the church about her insights and was rejected, her splinter group attracted people to a dangerous and one-sided view of the physical body and the material world. When the church stopped offering instructions on how to be quiet and meditate, it started people on a long, roundabout exploration of Eastern meditation and drugs—which at least shows their deep inner need for religious experience and altered states of consciousness. The failure to provide understanding about life after death and ways for people to relate that understanding to their lives encourages spiritualism and groups dedicated to it.

When people have deep and abiding experiences of God, ESP experiences often occur. Clairvoyance, telepathy, precognition, psychokinesis, and healing have been observed in and around the lives of many religious leaders and nearly all Christian saints. If these phenomena are not accepted and given a legitimate place in religious life, they will be sought outside of the church and for other than religious reasons. They are of questionable value when they are sought as ends in themselves rather than as part of an experience of God himself. This is true of any kind of human experience; separated entirely from the idea of expressing the love of God, almost anything we do can get mixed up with evil and be used for the wrong purposes.

142

Christians can understand ESP and see it as a natural capacity that can happen spontaneously and often becomes alive within deeply religious people. When ESP is seen in this light, religious people need not fear it. These experiences can be integrated into the fabric of our religious lives, giving them more depth and completeness and excitement and also making it harder for unwise separatist groups to spring up.

ESP is a natural phenomenon of the human psyche. It can be used for the glory of God and the enrichment of human life when it is understood and placed in the service of divine love, the love expressed in and through Jesus Christ. Religion shorn of these psi experiences becomes far more dull, and instead of attracting people, turns many of them away from the creative wholeness which is possible as God's people.

NOTES

1. The Reach of Human Knowing

1. Charles Panati, *Supersenses: Our Potential for Parasensory Experience*. (New York: Quadrangle/The New York Times Book Co., 1974), p. 12.

2. Book review by Urban T. Holmes III of Morton Kelsey, *Myth, History and Faith* in *St. Luke's Journal of Theology*, XVIII, No. 2 (March, 1975), p. 201.

3. F. R. Tennant, *Philosophical Theology* (Cambridge, England: Cambridge University Press, 1956), pp. 324f., also pp. 311f.

2. What Is ESP?

1. There are three excellent books which can be particularly recommended. The best general survey is *Supersenses*, published in 1974. The author, Charles Panati, is a physicist who has also written three other books on optics and digital communications.

Another work written from a scientific point of view is *Supernature* by Lyall Watson, a biologist who became interested in ESP because he realized that living things are far more in touch with their environment than sensory experience alone allows for. His book, brought out in 1973, provides a superb bibliography.

The Medium, the Mystic and the Physicist by Lawrence LeShan is written more from a theoretical point of view. LeShan is a research-oriented psychologist whose work led him to an interest in ESP phenomena. In this book, published in 1974, he is interested in trying to discover a theory or frame of reference which will help to explain these various phenomena.

In addition, in the issue of February 22, 1975, the *Saturday Review* carried a special section which offers a fine summary of the literature and developments in the field. Stanley Krippner's *Song of the Siren* gives one of the most recent accounts of the field by the well-known researcher.

2. *Mental Radio* was revised and brought out in 1962 by the scientific publishing house, Charles C. Thomas, and this edition is still in print, along with a paperback published by Macmillan Company in 1971. Two hundred and ninety of the tests are described in this book, of which almost a fourth were complete successes, over half were partial successes, and less than one-fourth failures.

The response to this book was fascinating, although limited to a few open minds like Sir Arthur Conan Doyle, Mahatma Gandhi, and Albert Einstein. Gandhi wrote that "nobody in India would, I think, doubt the possibility of [this kind of experience] but would doubt the wisdom of its material use," quoted in Mary Craig Sinclair, *Southern Belle* (New York: Crown Publishers, Inc., 1957), p. 319.

Einstein wrote an introduction to the German edition, and Mary Roberts Rinehart commented in one letter that people needed to appreciate the tremendous importance of the connotation of such experiences. Some of Mrs. Sinclair's other experiences, for instance one involving their friend Jack London, are told in her autobiography and in *The Autobiography of Upton Sinclair*.

3. Panati, p. 234.

4. An interpretation of this classic work of both religion and art is given by Helen Luke in her readable and profound *Dark Wood to White Rose* (Pecos, New Mexico: Dove Publications, 1975). This study of the meaning of the *Divine Comedy* for people's present-day lives makes this work accessible even for people who find the poem itself somewhat heavy going.

5. Arthur Ford, as told to Jerome Ellison, *The Life Beyond Death* (New York: G. P. Putnam's Sons, 1971), p. 204.

6. Karlis Osis, *Deathbed Observations by Physicians and Nurses* (New York: Parapsychology Foundation, 1961).

7. The best summary of Jung's studies in parapsychology is in Aniela Jaffe's book, *From the Life and Work of C. G. Jung.*

8. Some investigators would revise Rhine's statistical methods, but this would not change the central significance of his results. Some of the most interesting work has been done in analyzing how interest, individual preferences, and emotional factors affected the individual scores. It happened that the best results of all these dice tests were produced in a competitive experiment between four gamblers who believed in their luck and four divinity students who believed just as much in the power of prayer.

9. From an editorial written by J. B. Rhine; quoted in Louisa E. Rhine, *Mind Over Matter: Psychokinesis.* (New York: The Macmillan Company, 1970), p. 100. Also quoted in Lyall Watson, *Supernature: A Natural History of the Supernatural.*

10. Panati, p. 236.

11. *The Varieties of Healing Experience* and *The Dimensions of Healing* are published by the Academy of Parapsychology and Medicine, 314 Second Street, Los Altos, CA 94022.

12. This discussion is found at the end of his book *Persuasion and Healing.* Dr. Frank gives some of his most interesting evidence in discussing the removal of warts by suggestion. He tells about the highly sophisticated "double-blind" method of testing placebos against active medicines, an experimental method in which neither doctor nor patient knows whether the active pill or the placebo is being administered until the test is finished. Often, he shows, all that a patient needs is to be given an inert substance along with the belief that it is a pill or an ointment that will work. See Chapter 4, "The Placebo Effect and the Role of Expectations in Medical and Psychological Treatment," in *Persuasion and Healing.* Certainly hex doctors can do as well, and perhaps even better.

146

3. How We Experience ESP

1. Several recent books on dreams describe this new research method. In Chapters 1 and 8 of my book *God, Dreams, and Revelation* I have given a brief survey of these physiological studies and also of the work of modern psychologists. In addition I have tried to show the dream theories of the Old Testament, the New Testament, and the early church, then tracing the beliefs about dreams in the later history of Christianity.

2. These are Montague Ullman and Stanley Krippner, *Dream Studies and Telepathy: An Experimental Approach* (New York: Parapsychological Foundation, Inc., 1970). Also Montague Ullman, et al., *Dream Telepathy* (New York: The Macmillian Company, 1973).

3. Jacques Hadamard has detailed many examples of unconscious intuitions which have led to scientific discovery. This is reported in the *Conférence faite au Palais de la Découverte le 8 Décembre 1945* (W. D. Alençon). The same author has written *The Psychology of Invention in the Mathematical Field* (New York: Dover Publications, Inc., 1945).

4. Andrew Greeley has done a sociological survey of mystical experiences and finds that they are quite common among ordinary people. This work is reported in his article "Are We a Nation of Mystics?", in the magazine section of *The New York Times* for January 27, 1975.

5. The data on these experiments are found in Claudio Naranjo and Robert E. Ornstein, *On the Psychology of Meditation* (New York: The Viking Press, 1972), pp. 163ff.

6. C. G. Jung, *Memories, Dreams, Reflections*, recorded and ed. by Aniela Jaffé (New York: Pantheon Books, 1963), p. 316. Aniela Jaffé's *From the Life and Work of C. G. Jung* (New York: Harper & Row, 1971), offers a great deal of carefully gathered detail about Jung's interest in the whole field of parapsychology, much of it tucked away in letters and other sources and hard to locate.

7. Lyall Watson, *Supernature*, gives a delightful list of systems of divination. See p. 268.

4. ESP in the Bible and Church History

1. In *Healing and Christianity*, I have discussed the differ-ence between the two points of view at some length. See pp. 33ff. and 88ff.

2. James Hastings' *Dictionary of the Bible* gives a careful outline of the various experiences. See the articles on Magic, Divination, Sorcery, and on Urim and Thummim.

3. See J. R. Pridie, *The Spiritual Gifts* (London: Robert Scott, 1921), for a careful discussion of these gifts; also, my book on *Tongue Speaking*.

4. A longer account of Augustine's sophisticated theory of knowing, with the references given in the footnotes, and also a similar outline of the point of view of Gregory of Nyssa can be found in my book *God, Dreams, and Revelation*, pp. 148ff. and 133ff. Similar accounts of their thinking in regard to healing are found in my book *Healing and Christianity*, pp. 184ff. and 171ff. In addition, the original edition of *God, Dreams, and Revelation* included certain of Augustine's letters in which he described and discussed at length various ESP experiences in dreams.

5. Understanding Psi

1. I am deeply grateful for the wisdom of James Kirsch in opening the door of understanding for me to hear what Jung was saying. Victor White's *God and the Unconscious* also helped to make clear Jung's point about the reality of the psychoid or spiritual world. For the student who wishes to know more about Jung's thinking in this regard, his article on "Synchronicity: An Acausal Connecting Principle" (in Vol. 8 of the *Collected Works*), is a must.

2. I have considered the theories of evil in more detail in my book *Myth, History and Faith*, and also in the pamphlet published by Dove Publications, Pecos, New Mexico, *The Reality of the Spiritual World*, as well as in articles on "The Mythology of Evil" in the *Journal of Religion and Health*, Vol. 13, No. 1, 1974, and on "Aggression and Religion: The Psychology and Theology of the Punitive Element in Man" in *Religious Education*, Vol. 68, No. 3, 1973.

A world view which sees the universe as basically understandable in terms of cause and effect (the view of Aristotle and the Scholastics) makes the phenomena of ESP either supernatural or demonic. Jeffrey Burton Russell in his authoritative study, *Witchcraft in the Middle Ages* (Cornell University Press, 1972, pp. 142-143), has stated this superbly:

"Just as important, they [the Scholastics] generally adopted an Aristotelian world view favoring the development of witchcraft as opposed to a Neoplatonic world view favoring the development of high magic and not as conducive to witch beliefs. Neoplatonism, vigorously combated by most scholastics, did not regain its position until the Renaissance. The Neoplatonic view was that a world soul united the universe in one system of microcosm-macrocosm, sympathy-antipathy, so that all things were interrelated and mutually responsive. In such a universe any marvel could be effected through natural magic without recourse to the supernatural. Such a view was adopted by Neoplatonist Renaissance magicians like Giordano Bruno and by most of the modern occultists that succeeded them. This adherence to natural magic partially explains the traditional antipathy of occultists toward supernatural religion.

"Natural magic, as Sir Walter Raleigh, one of its advocates, put it, 'Bringeth to light the inmost virtues, and draweth them out of Nature's hidden bosome to humane use: Virtutes in centro centri latentes: Virtues hidden in the center of the center.' As opposed to this approach, St. Thomas' view was set within a fundamentally Aristotelian framework, that is, a framework which assumed contact-action as the basis of efficient causation, ruled out action at a distance through sympathy-antipathy and the world-soul, and was inhospitable to the notion of marvelous effects being produced through 'natural' means. The Aquinian view, in other words, had the corollary that the extraordinary use of 'natural' laws to produce extraordinary effects in nature was only possible through demonic intervention. The Aristotelianism of the scholastics was a narrowly rational system, so that irrational events were seen as supernatural and often demonic. This was opposed to the more supple, mystical Neoplatonic system, which was broader in its acceptance of what was natural. Scholastic Aristotelianism was accordingly bound to reinforce the trend, already begun within the Augustinian tradition, toward driving magic in the direction of witchcraft."

149

6. ESP, Theology, and Christian Living

1. These stories are found in Matthew 17:24-27; Matthew 21:1-11, Mark 11:1-11, Luke 19:29-40; Mark 14:12-16, Luke 22:7-13; and the references to Jesus' predictions of his death and resurrection occur in Matthew 9:14-15, 16:21-22, 17:9-12, 22-23, 20:17-19, 26:1-2, and 21; in Mark 2:18-20, 8:31, 9:9, 31, 10:32-34, 14:17-18, and 28; in Luke 5:33-35, 9:21-22, 43-44, 12:49-50, 18:31-33, 22:14-16, and 21-22; and in John 6:64, 7:33-34, 12:23-33, 13:1, 21-27, 14:18-19, 28, 16:5, 16, 28, and 18:32.

Extrasensory Experiences in the New Testament

The following extrasensory experiences of Jesus, his disciples, and others close to him are found in the gospels in the passages indicated:

KNOWLEDGE (clairvoyant, precognitive or telepathic) given in various ways:

	MATT.	MARK	LUKE	JOHN
that his wife would conceive and bear a son (John the Baptist), given to Zechariah by an angel in a vision			1:8-25	
of Elizabeth's pregnancy, given to Mary by an angel in a vision			1:36-37	
that she herself would conceive by the Holy Spirit and bear a son, to be named Jesus, given to Mary by an angel in a vision			1:26-35	
that Mary was pregnant by the Holy Spirit, given to Joseph by an angel in a dream	1:20-25			
of the birth of Christ the Lord, given to shepherds by an angel in a vision			2:10-18	
of the birth of the Christ, given to the wise men through a star	2:1-11			
of Herod's intentions, given to the wise men by God in a dream	2:12			
of Herod's intentions, given to Joseph by an angel in a dream	2:13-15			
of Herod's death, given to Joseph by an angel in a dream	2:19-21			
of danger in Judaea, given to Joseph by God in a dream	2:22-23			
that he would see the Christ before he died, given to Simeon by the Holy Spirit			2:25-35	
and wisdom given to the child Jesus			2:46-50	
of the Spirit of God descending upon Jesus, seen as a dove and heard as a voice	3:16-17	1:9-11	3:21-22	
as seen and heard by John the Baptist				1:32-34

	MATT.	MARK	LUKE	JOHN
of the devil, given to Jesus	4:1-11	1:12-13	4:1-13	
of demons, given to Jesus		1:23-25 1:34 3:11-12	4:33-35 4:41	
	8:30-32	5:8-13	8:29-33	
about Nathanael, given to Jesus				1:47-51
that a sick person had touched his cloak, given to Jesus		5:27-33	8:45-47	
of the secret thoughts of the scribes and Pharisees, given to Jesus	9:3-6 12:24-26	2:6-9	5:21-23 6:7-9 7:39-43	
about the woman at the well in Samaria, given to Jesus				4:16-19
that Peter and his companions would net a huge number of fish, given to Jesus			5:4-10	
of Jesus being touched and spoken to from heaven, given to Peter, John and James in a vision	17:1-8	9:2-8	9:28-36	12:28-30
—given to a crowd of people				
that Peter would catch a fish with a coin in its mouth, given to Jesus	17:24-27			
of how the two disciples would find a donkey and colt, or a colt never yet ridden, given to Jesus	21:1-7	11:1-7	19:29-35	
that Peter and John would find a man carrying water who would lead them to a house with an upper room suitable for the Passover supper, given to Jesus		14:12-16	22:7-13	
of the suffering about to be inflicted on Jesus, given to Pilate's wife in a dream	27:19			

PREDICTIONS made by Jesus (indicating specifically precognitive experiences):

	MATT.	MARK	LUKE	JOHN
of his betrayal, death, and resurrection	9:14-15 16:21-22	2:18-20 8:31-32	5:33-35 9:21-22	2:18-22 6:64, 70-1 7:33-34

				30-35
	17:22-23	9:30-32	9:43-45	
			12:50	
			13:32-33	
	20:17-19, 22	10:32-34, 38	18:31-34	
	26:1-2			
	26:20-25, 29	14:17-21, 25	22:21-23, 14-18	13:21-27
				13:1
	26:32	14:28		14:18-19, 28-30
	26:45-46	14:41-42		
				16:5, 16, 28
that Peter would deny knowing him three times before	26:32-35, 56, 58, 69-75	14:29-31, 54, 66-72	22:31-34, 54-62	13:37-38
				18:15-18, 25-27

DIRECT PSYCHIC OR SPIRITUAL EFFECTS UPON MATERIAL THINGS (psychokinetic effects):

Zechariah's speech affected by the vision of an angel			1:20-22, 59-64	
water changed into wine by Jesus				2:1-11
the wind and sea calmed by Jesus	8:23-27	4:35-41	8:22-25	
food provided for the crowds of people by Jesus	14:15-21 / 15:32-38	6:35-44 / 8:1-9	9:12-17	6:5-14
Jesus walks on water	14:24-33	6:47-52		6:16-21
a barren fig tree is withered by Jesus	21:18-22	11:12-14, 20-23		
Jesus' crucifixion brings darkness over the land	27:45	15:33	23:44-45	
Jesus' crucifixion rends the veil of the Temple	27:51	15:38	23:45	
Jesus' crucifixion causes the earth to quake	27:51-54			
effect on the time of Jesus' death		15:44-45	23:46-47	
the stone rolled away and the tomb empty	28:1-2	16:2-4	24:1-3	19:28-30, 32-33
				20:1-2

PHYSICAL AND MENTAL HEALINGS DONE BY JESUS:

	MATT.	MARK	LUKE	JOHN
of man with an unclean spirit		1:21-28	4:33-37	
of Peter's mother-in-law	8:14-15	1:30-31	4:38-39	
of a leper	8:2-4	1:40-45	5:12-15	
of a centurion's servant	8:5-13		7:2-10	
of a court official's son				4:46-54
of a man who had been an invalid for 38 years				5:2-16
of a paralytic	9:2-9	2:3-12	5:17-26	
of a demoniac (or demoniacs) of Gadara	8:28-34	5:1-20	8:26-40	
of Jairus' daughter	9:18-19, 23-26	5:22-24, 35-43	8:41-42, 49-56	
of the woman with a hemorrhage	9:20-22	5:25-34	8:43-48	
of a man with a withered hand	12:9-13	3:1-5	6:6-10	
of two blind men	9:27-31			
of a widow's son in Nain			7:11-17	
of a dumb demoniac	9:32-33		11:14	
of Mary Magdalene, Joanna, Susanna, and many others			8:2-4	
of a blind and dumb demoniac	12:22-23			
of a Canaanite woman's daughter	15:22-28	7:25-30		
of a deaf man with an impediment in his speech		7:32-37		
of a blind man		8:22-26		
of an epileptic child with an evil spirit	17:14-21	9:14-29	9:37-43	
of a crippled woman			13:10-13	
of a man with dropsy			14:2-4	
of ten lepers			17:12-19	
of a man born blind				9:1-39
of a blind man (Bartimaeus) or two blind men	20:29-34	10:46-52	18:35-43	
of Lazarus				11:1-45
of Malchus' ear (servant of the High Priest)			22:49-51	
of a few sick folk	13:58	6:5-6	6:17-19	
of great numbers of people	4:23-25	1:32-34	4:40-41	
	8:16-17	1:39	5:15	
	9:35-36			

	11:4-5	3:9-12	7:21-22	
	12:15-16		9:11	6:2
	14:13-14	6:54-56		
	14:35-36			
	15:30-31		13:32	
	19:2			
similar power given to the disciples to heal	21:14-15 10:1	6:7-13 3:14-15	9:1-6	
—to the seventy others	10:7-8	6:30	9:10 10:1, 9 10:17-20	
power of others to cast out demons in the name of Jesus		9:38-39	9:49-50	
RESURRECTION APPEARANCES:				
foretold by an angel or angels —by finding the empty tomb	28:1-7	16:1-8	24:1-12	20:1-10
to Mary Magdalene (and the "other Mary")	28:9-10	16:9-11*		20:11-18
to Cleopas and another, or two others		16:12-13*	24:13-35	
to the eleven disciples	28:16-20	16:14-20*	24:36-53	20:19-25, 26-29
to the disciples at the Lake of Tiberias				21:1-22
also, of Moses and Elijah to Peter, John and James	17:3-4	9:4-5	9:30-33	
of many holy men to a number of people	27:52-53			

* From the addition to Mark. These verses, however, appear to come from a very early source.

Similar experiences of the apostles are found in the following places in Acts:

KNOWLEDGE, wisdom, instruction—given in clairvoyant, precognitive or telepathic experiences:

	Acts
about the Holy Spirit and what would happen, given to the group by Jesus	1:6-8
about Jesus' ascension and how he would return, given to the group by two angels	1:9-11
about the lie told by Ananias and Sapphira, given to Peter	5:3-4
of heaven, Jesus and God, given to Stephen in a vision	7:55-56, 59
about where to go next, given to Philip by an angel of the Lord	8:26
about what he must do, given to Paul by Jesus in a vision	9:3-8, 22:6-11, 26:12-20
about finding and healing Paul, given to Ananias by the Lord in a vision	9:10-16, 22:14-15
about Ananias and being healed by him, given to Paul by the Lord in a vision	9:11-12
about Peter and where to find him, given to Cornelius by an angel in a vision	10:1-8, 30-33
about eating gentile food, given to Peter by God in a trance-vision	10:9-17, 28-29 11:5-10
about the men standing at the door, given to Peter by the Spirit	10:17-23, 11:11-14
about baptizing Cornelius and his friends, given to Peter and the others by the Holy Spirit through hearing ecstatic speech	10:44-48, 11:15-18
about starting Paul and Barnabas on their mission, given to certain prophets by the Holy Spirit	13:1-4
about going to Macedonia, given to Paul in a dream	16:9-11
about speaking out with confidence, given to Paul by the Lord in a vision	18:9-11
about leaving Jerusalem, given to Paul by God in a trance-vision	22:17-21

PREDICTIONS (specifically precognitive experiences):

	ACTS
of a famine over the whole empire, given to the prophet Agabus by the Spirit	11:27-30
of imprisonment and persecution, given to Paul by the Holy Spirit	20:22-26
of Paul's imprisonment, given to the prophet Agabus by the Holy Spirit	21:10-14
that he would live to reach Rome, given to Paul by the Lord in a dream	23:11
that their ship would be wrecked and lost, but without loss of life, given to Paul by an angel of God	27:21-26, 31-36, 42-44

DIRECT PSYCHIC OR SPIRITUAL EFFECTS ON MATERIAL THINGS (psychokinetic effects):

the apostles' speech affected as they are filled with the Holy Spirit	2:1-13
the house shaken as the apostles pray and are filled with the Holy Spirit	4:31-33
Ananias and Sapphira struck down because of their lie	5:1-11
the apostles released from prison by an angel of the Lord	5:19-26
Philip taken away from where his mission was completed by the Spirit of the Lord	8:38-40
Paul left blinded by his vision on the Damascus Road	9:8-9
Peter delivered from prison by an angel of the Lord	12:4-12
Herod struck down by an angel of the Lord	12:21-23
the Jewish magician Elymas temporarily blinded by the Lord for interfering	13:6-12
Paul and Silas released from prison by an earthquake	16:25-35
speech of the disciples at Ephesus affected by the Holy Spirit	19:5-7
the seven sons of Sceva mauled by an evil spirit	19:13-20

PHYSICAL AND MENTAL HEALINGS:

of a cripple by Peter and John	3:1-16
of Paul's eyesight by Ananias	9:17-19, 22:12-16
of the paralyzed Aeneas by Peter	9:33-35
Tabitha (Dorcas) brought back to life by Peter	9:36-42
of a lame man by Paul	14:8-11
spirit (of divination) cast out of a slave girl by Paul	16:16-19
Eutychus brought back to life by Paul	20:7-12
of Paul from snake-bite	28:3-6
of Publius' father from dysentery and fever by Paul	28:7-8
of numbers of people, by the apostles	2:43*
	5:12*
by Peter	5:15-16
by Stephen	6:8*
by Philip	8:6-8*
	8:13*
by Paul and Barnabas	14:3*
	15:12*
by Paul	19:11-12
	28:9

In addition, there are various other appearances of angels or of the Holy Spirit in the gospels and Acts, other predictions of the future made by Jesus, and also other passages which reveal or suggest the exceptional wisdom and knowledge (of things both in heaven and on earth) that were given to Jesus and others around him.

---

* For the use of the Greek words for miracles, works of power or mighty works, and signs and wonders to indicate healings, see my book *Healing and Christianity*, pp. 105 ff.

BIBLIOGRAPHY

A. ESP Research

Charles Panati, *Supersenses: Our Potential for Parasensory Experience*. New York: Quadrangle/The New York Times Book Co., 1974. The most complete factual survey of recent research in this field. Panati's style is readable and he allows the experiences to speak for themselves.

Lyall Watson, *Supernature: A Natural History of the Supernatural*. New York: Bantam Books, Inc., 1974. Another thorough study of the research with somewhat more emphasis on the biological aspects and the meaning for human life.

Lawrence LeShan, *The Medium, the Mystic, and the Physicist: Toward a General Theory of the Paranormal*. New York: The Viking Press, 1974. LeShan examines attitudes towards ESP, explores one area of experimentation, and seeks to understand the metaphysical basis of these experiences.

Stanley Krippner, *Song of the Siren: A Parapsychological Odyssey*. New York: Harper & Row, 1975. A fascinating insight into the problems faced by early psi researchers and how the data kept leading them on.

Jeffrey Burton Russell, *Witchcraft in the Middle Ages*, Ithaca: Cornell University Press, 1972. This is the sanest and most authoritative discussion of the phenomenon of witchcraft and demonism yet written.

B. Toward a New World View

Thomas S. Kuhn, *The Structure of Scientific Revolutions*. 2nd ed. Chicago: The University of Chicago Press, 1970.

Werner Heisenberg, *Physics and Philosophy: The Revolution in Modern Science*. New York: Harper and Brothers, 1958.

By mapping the process of scientific change, Kuhn shows how new facts are revealed and thus comes to a new view of the world. Heisenberg details how the changes came about in modern physics, and how this new understanding can open up a new view of reality.

Alfred Jules Ayer, *Language, Truth and Logic*. New York: Dover Publications,, Inc., 1952.

Kenneth G. Johnson, *General Semantics: An Outline Survey*. (Pamphlet.) Madison: University of Wisconsin Extension

Division, 1960. Two indispensable works delineating the uses and limitations of language and logic in our search for knowledge.

Arthur O. Lovejoy, *The Revolt Against Dualism.* New York: W. W. Norton & Company, Inc., 1930. This brilliant study of human knowing opens the door to a broader view of how knowledge is acquired than is usually recognized in our culture.

Lancelot Law Whyte, *The Unconscious before Freud.* New York: Basic Books, Inc., 1960. A survey of the twisting path towards recognition of a realm of largely unconscious experience and the questions that have thus been opened up.

C. G. Jung, *Memories, Dreams, Reflections.* Recorded and edited by Aniela Jaffé. New York: Pantheon Books, 1963. This psychiatrist tells of his struggles in coming to understand the unconscious and in finding meaning for himself.

C. G. Jung, *Modern Man in Search of a Soul.* New York: Harcourt, Brace and Company, 1933. ——, *Analytical Psychology: Its Theory and Practice.* New York: Random House, 1968. ——, *Two Essays on Analytical Psychology.* New York: World Publishing Co., 1956. Jung offers a penetrating look at the need of modern men and women to know the unconscious and the realm of spirit. He draws on a great wealth of experience with people to illustrate how this knowledge is found, the kind of things that are revealed, and some of the reasons it is valuable for individuals to experience and relate to these phenomena.

Andrew Weil, *The Natural Mind: A New Way of Looking at Drugs and the Higher Consciousness.* Boston: Houghton Mifflin Company, 1973. Weil suggests that we will not begin to solve the growing drug problem until we are ready to deal with the need for altered states of consciousness.

John Macquarrie, *Twentieth-Century Religious Thought: The Frontiers of Philosophy and Theology, 1900-1960.* New York: Harper & Row, 1963. A careful survey of over 150 modern theological thinkers which demonstrates the lack of confidence of modern theology in the value of religious experience.

Victor White, *God and the Unconscious.* Cleveland: The World Publishing Company, 1961. A well-known Roman

Catholic theologian personally acquainted with Jung, discusses the religious implications of Jung for religious thought.

David B. Burrell, *Exercises in Religious Understanding*. Notre Dame, Indiana: University of Notre Dame Press, 1975. A penetrating and careful analysis of man's language in discussing the divine which includes a philosophical interpretation of Jung's religious language and understanding.

Morton T. Kelsey, *Encounter with God*. Minneapolis: Bethany Fellowship, Inc., 1972. ——, *The Reality of the Spiritual World*. Pecos, New Mexico: Dove Publications, 1974. An attempt to show reasons for believing that God and spiritual realities can touch men and women through the depth of the psyche or soul, bringing changes in their consciousness, and also in their bodies and sometimes in other kinds of matter.

C. G. Jung, "Synchronicity: An Acausal Connecting Principle," *Collected Works*, Vol. 8. 2nd ed. Princeton, N.J.: Princeton University Press, 1969. Presents Jung's understanding that there is meaning in many coincidences.

Aniela Jaffé, *From the Life and Work of C. G. Jung*. New York: Harper & Row, 1971. Further understanding of Jung's view of ESP phenomena and of the principle of synchronicity as providing "a basis for a new answer to the philosophical question of a world order."

C. Psi Phenomena

Upton Sinclair, *Mental Radio*. Rev. ed. Springfield, Ill.: Charles C. Thomas, 1962. Detailed descriptions of 425 experiments in telepathy and clairvoyance. An early example of careful study and reporting.

Vincent and Margaret Gaddis, *The Curious World of Twins*. New York: Hawthorne Books, Inc., 1971. Examples of telepathic communication between twins, exploring the close relationship even to spontaneous similarity of changes in brain waves.

Berthold E. Schwarz, *Parent-Child Telepathy: A Study of the Telepathy of Everyday Life*. New York: Garrett Publications-Helix Press, 1973. Further studies of how the telepathic influences break through when there are close relationships between individuals.

Montague Ullman and Stanley Krippner, *Dream Studies and*

Telepathy: An Experimental Approach. New York: Parapsychology Foundation, Inc., 1970. An important breakthrough in scientifically controlled research into telepathy.

Louisa E. Rhine, *E S P in Life and Lab.* New York: The Macmillan Company, 1967. ——, *Mind Over Matter: Psychokinesis.* New York: The Macmillan Company, 1970. Significant insights into the lives and work of the researchers who first tried to apply scientific methods to the study of ESP.

Sheila Ostrander and Lynn Schroeder, *Psychic Discoveries Behind the Iron Curtain.* Englewood Cliffs, N.J.: Prentice-Hall, Inc., 1970. Covers the Soviet interest in parapsychology from the development of Kirlian photography to the possible uses of telepathy and the estimated budget for research at that time.

C. D. Broad, *Lectures on Psychical Research.* London: Routledge & Kegan Paul, 1962. Includes some of the extremely important experiments by Dr. S. G. Soal and a variety of dream, out-of-the-body, and mediumistic experiences.

Charles T. Tart, Ed., *Altered States of Consciousness.* New York: John Wiley & Sons, Inc., 1969. An inquiry into ways of altering consciousness such as biofeedback, dreaming, self-hypnosis, etc.

Morton T. Kelsey, *God, Dreams, and Revelation: A Christian Interpretation of Dreams.* Minneapolis: Augsburg Publishing House, 1974. ——, *Tongue Speaking: An Experiment in Spiritual Experience.* Garden City, N.Y.: Doubleday & Company, Inc., 1964. These books try to offer understanding of the ESP phenomena sometimes occurring along with dreams and the experience of tongue speaking.

Frances G. Wickes, *The Inner World of Childhood.* New York: The New American Library, Inc., 1968. A report on the reality of the child's world of dreams and imaginary playmates.

C. G. Jung, *Collected Works.* Princeton, N.J.: Princeton University Press, various dates. Also, *Memories, Dreams, Reflections* (cited in Section B). Discussions of various ESP experiences are found all through Jung's works.

Jane Roberts, *The Seth Material.* Englewood Cliffs, N.J.: Prentice-Hall, Inc., 1970. ——, *Seth Speaks: The Eternal Validity of the Human Soul.* Englewood Cliffs, N.J.: Prentice-Hall, Inc., 1972. Records of a woman's contacts with a masculine personality who spoke through her in a distinctly different voice, dictating many discussions of ESP abilities and sometimes giving precognitive information.

Robert A. Monroe, *Journeys Out of the Body*. Garden Cty, N.Y.: Doubleday & Company, Inc., 1971. A glimpse into another world of experience. Monroe is convinced that the people, places and events he meets on a spiritual plane are as real as his physical life.

Karlis Osis, *Deathbed Observations by Physicians and Nurses.* New York: Parapsychology Foundation, Inc., 1961. The experiences of dying patients give evidence of the reality of life after death.

James A. Pike with Diane Kennedy, *The Other Side: An Account of My Experiences with Psychic Phenomena.* Garden City, N.Y.: Doubleday & Company, Inc., 1968. An amazing revelation of the psi events surrounding the death of Bishop Pike's son.

Arthur Ford, as told to Jerome Ellison, *The Life Beyond Death.* New York: G. P. Putnam's Sons, 1971. Summarizes the various beliefs about life after death and discusses a number of the studies and psychic experiences which support that belief.

D. Healing

The Varieties of Healing Experience: Exploring Psychic Phenomena in Healing and *The Dimensions of Healing: A Symposium.* Los Altos, California: The Academy of Parapsychology and Medicine, 1971 and 1972. Reports of conferences on psychic healing covering many aspects from some of the most carefully controlled research to the imaginative and successful combination of medical, psychological and spiritual treatment of Carl Simonton.

Hugh L. Cayce, *Venture Inward.* New York: Harper & Row, 1964. Thomas Sugrue, *There Is a River.* Rev. ed. New York: Holt, Rinehart and Winston, 1942. The story of Edgar Cayce, his life, and the healings that resulted from his trance utterances.

John G. Fuller, *Arigo: Surgeon of the Rusty Knife.* New York: Pocket Books, 1975. An investigation of an uneducated Brazilian healer whose diagnosis and sophisticated prescriptions, primitive surgery and cures performed in a trance state baffle any attempt at rational explanation.

163

Herbert Benson, *The Relaxation Response*. New York: William Morrow & Company, Inc., 1975. Presents ways of using meditation to alter our tension-stress reactions and find healthier functioning of body and mind.

Barbara B. Brown, *New Mind, New Body: Bio-Feedback: New Directions for the Mind*. New York: Harper & Row, 1974. Describes research with monitoring devices to "teach" control of a specific body function, such as heart rate, blood pressure, temperature of hands or feet, or brain wave pattern.

Jerome D. Frank, *Persuasion and Healing*. New York: Schocken Books, 1963. A leading professor of psychiatry writes about religious factors in healing and the need to consider such elements in treating patients.

Agnes Sanford, *The Healing Light*. St. Paul: Macalester Park Publishing Co., 1947. The basic primer of spiritual or Christian healing.

Francis MacNutt, *Healing*. Notre Dame, Indiana: Ave Maria Press, 1974. An important introduction to the practice of Christian healing and to understanding the relation to other facets of life.

Morton T. Kelsey, *Healing and Christianity*. New York: Harper & Row, 1973. An attempt to show historically, psychologically, and in relation to modern medical practice the meaning that spiritual healing can have for modern Christians.

E. Mythology

Morton T. Kelsey, *Myth, History and Faith: The Remythologizing of Christianity*. New York: Paulist Press, 1974. A study of the living reality of religious myths, the process by which myths can become actual history, and the importance of myth, particularly the Christian myth, for our history and our present-day lives.

Carl G. Jung, Ed., *Man and His Symbols*. Garden City, N.Y.: Doubleday & Company, Inc., 1964. A graphic and easy to read presentation of the meaning of mythological symbols for human beings.

John A. Sanford, *The Man Who Wrestled With God*. King of Prussia, Pa.: Religious Publishing Co., 1974. The stories of Jacob, Joseph, and Adam and Eve are brought to life with as much meaning and reality for people today as these symbolic events had for the ancient Hebrews.

——, *The Kingdom Within: A Study of the Inner Meaning of Jesus' Sayings*. Philadelphia: J. B. Lippincott Company, 1970. Reveals the mythological quality of the parables of the kingdom of God, showing how their images can help individuals find in their own lives the meaning expressed by Jesus.

Margaret Brown, *The Bible's Nuclear Energy*. King of Prussia, Pa.: Religious Publishing Co., 1975. Illustrates how the stories and miracles and the life of Jesus can lead a person to seek for wholeness and find the power that is available to us in this Christian experience.

Walter Wink, *The Bible in Human Transformation: Toward a New Paradigm for Biblical Study*. Philadelphia: Fortress Press, 1975. Offers a method for using the Bible as a living myth to bring growth and development in our own lives.

Helen M. Luke, *Dark Wood to White Rose: A Study of Meanings in Dante's Divine Comedy*. Pecos, N.M.: Dove Publications, 1975. Dante and his guides, Virgil and later Beatrice, point out the way of integration as they follow each experience from hell to the highest heaven.

Robert Johnson, *He!*. King of Prussia, Pa.: Religious Publishing Co., 1974. ——, *She!*. King of Prussia, Pa.: Religious Publishing Co., 1976. The myth of Parsifal's search for the Grail gives an approach to masculine development, and the way of feminine development is opened up through the story of Amor and Psyche.

Joseph Campbell, *The Hero with a Thousand Faces*. New York: Meridian Books, 1956. ——, *Myths to Live By*. New York: Viking Press, 1972. The myths of many religions and cultures are used to explore the path of human growth and wholeness.

Heinrich Zimmer, *The King and the Corpse: Tales of the Soul's Conquest of Evil*. Joseph Campbell, Ed. Princeton, N.J.: Princeton University Press, 1971. Three of the world's great folk tales help to reveal the reality of evil and some of the ways of dealing with it.

James Kallas, *The Real Satan: From Biblical Times to the Present*. Minneapolis: Augsburg Publishing House, 1975. Makes the reality of Satan clear, and also the fact that our only real protection comes from the spirit of God as evidenced by the person of Jesus Christ.

Heinrich Zimmer, *Myths and Symbols in Indian Art and Civilization.* Joseph Campbell, Ed. New York: Harper & Row, 1962. Zimmer concludes his study of Far Eastern myths with a delightful Hassidic tale illustrating that one may have to travel far to find where to look for treasure. But in the end the treasure will be found at home, buried in an odd corner of our own history and myths and beliefs.

F. Religious Experiences

The basic work on the experiences of premodern or "primitive" religions—the dreams, visions, experiences of dismemberment (those of the "wounded healer"), healings, and all kinds of ESP experiences—is:

Mircea Eliade, *Shamanism: Archaic Technique of Ecstasy.* Princeton, N.J.: Princeton University Press, 1970.

Similar experiences found among the American Indians are described in:

John G. Neihardt, *Black Elk Speaks: Being the Life Story of a Holy Man of the Oglala Sioux.* Lincoln: University of Nebraska Press, 1961.

Lame Deer and Richard Erdoes, *Lame Deer: Seeker of Visions.* New York: Simon and Schuster, 1972.

Franc Johnson Newcomb, *Hosteen Klah: Navaho Medicine Man and Sand Painter.* Norman: University of Oklahoma Press, 1964.

David Villasenor, *Tapestries in Sand: The Spirit of Indian Sandpainting.* Healdsburg, Calif.: Naturegraph Company, 1966.

Many of the same experiences and the search for them are elaborated and discussed in:

Carlos Castaneda, *The Teachings of Don Juan: A Yaqui Way of Knowledge.* Berkeley: University of California Press, 1968.

———, *A Separate Reality: Further Conversations with Don Juan.* New York: Simon and Schuster, 1971.

———, *Journey to Ixtlan: The Lessons of Don Juan.* New York: Pocket Books, 1974.

———, *Tales of Power.* New York: Simon and Schuster, 1974.

166

Scientists speak of religious experience:

C. G. Jung, *Memories, Dreams, Reflections,* (cited in Section B), describes the psychologist's contacts with another realm, including his experiences of death and his final reflection on Eros (or love) as the source of all our being and becoming.

Claudio Naranjo and Robert E. Ornstein, *On the Psychology of Meditation.* New York: The Viking Press, 1971. An analysis of Zen, Yoga, and other ways of surrender, awareness and self-expression.

The Christian experience is described in the classic works by

Baron Friedrich von Hügel, *The Mystical Element of Religion as Studied in Saint Catherine of Genoa and Her Friends.* London: J. M. Dent & Sons Limited, 1927.

————, *Eternal Life.* Edinburgh: T. & T. Clark, 1912.

Also, Morton Kelsey, *The Other Side of Silence: A Guide to Christian Meditation.* New York: Paulist Press, 1976.

————, *Encounter with God* (cited in Section B). These two books describe in detail the most basic religious experiences which can come to Christians.

G. Liberal and Conservative Literature on ESP

Voices from His Excellent Glory. Book, Tape and Video Tape Library, Box 4174, Panorama City, California 91412. This gives a good and up-to-date survey of the field.

Don Basham, *Deliver Us from Evil.* Washington Depot, Connecticut 06794, Chosen Books, 1972.

Nicky Cruz, *Satan on the Loose.* Old Tappen, New Jersey, Fleming H. Revell Company, 1973.

Hobart E. Freeman, *Angels of Light?* Plainfield, New Jersey, Logos International, 1969.

Robert Frost, Ph.D., *Overflowing Life.* Plainfield, New Jersey, Logos International, 1971.

Raphael Gasson, *Challenging Counterfeit.* Plainfield, New Jersey, Logos, International, 1966.

Kenneth Hagin, *Demons and How to Deal with Them.* P.O. Box 50126, Tulsa, Oklahoma 74150. Also, *Ministering to the Oppressed, Authority of the Believer, Prayer Secrets, Right and Wrong Thinking, What Faith Is.*

Michael Harper, *Spiritual Warfare.* Watchung, New Jersey 07060, Charisma Books, 1970.

Donald R. Jacobs, *Demons*. Scottdale, Pennsylvania 15683, Herald Press, 1972.

Hal Lindsey, *Satan Is Alive and Well on Planet Earth*. Grand Rapids, Michigan 49506, Zondervan Publishing House 1972.

Bob Mumford, *Take Another Look at Guidance*. Plainfield, New Jersey, Logos, International, 1971.

Christopher Neil-Smith, *The Exorcist and the Possessed*. New York, Pinnacle Books, Inc., 1974.

John P. Newport, *Demons, Demons, Demons*. Nashville, Tennessee, Broadman Press, 1972.

Derek Prince, *Seven Ways to Keep Your Deliverance*. Tape, P.O. Box 306, Fort Lauderdale, Florida 33302, 1971. He lists several tapes on this subject.

Pete Underwood, *Deeper Into the Occult*. New York, Harrap Books, 1975.

Mike Warnke, *The Satan-Sellers*. Plainfield, New Jersey, Logos International, 1972.